Helping Your Business Grow

Helping Your Business Grow

101 Dynamic Ideas in Marketing

Brooks Fenno

amacom American Management Associations

Library of Congress Cataloging in Publication Data

Fenno, Brooks.
    Helping your business grow.

    Includes index.
    1. Marketing management. I. Title.
HF5415.13.F46   1982   658.8   82-71310
ISBN 0-8144-5733-9   AACR2

First Printing

Preface

The 101 ideas on which this book is based were derived from my experiences with many different companies over the past twenty years. They apply to a wide range of marketing problems and opportunities, from identifying customers to funding a start-up operation, but the reader will discern that all the ideas point to a single objective: *growth*.

This book is for readers who are looking for ways to make a company grow in an accelerated and orderly fashion. Just one of the ideas might do the trick, paying back your investment in the book a hundred times over. But for many the value of the book may well be in its presentation of marketing as a total concept, working effectively in every aspect of a business.

The time has surely come for small and medium-size businesses to take full advantage of the successful marketing strategies and techniques that have so long been the province of larger corporations. My book shows how this can be done. It does so in practical terms, with case histories and examples to illustrate concepts. Wherever possible, I have included material readily adaptable for use—forms, charts, sample letters, job descriptions, and so on.

It goes without saying that running a business demands hard work and commitment. It's fun, too—but never more so than when you meet your growth goals and your company prospers. If that's what you want, this book can help. Good luck!

ACKNOWLEDGMENTS

All the inspiration and most of the material for this book comes from my clients, past and present. I thank them here collectively.

For help in the writing, my thanks go to Joseph Callanan, whose editorial talents contributed greatly to the organization and flow of the text; to Georges Doriot, who helped me formulate a number of the key ideas; to Jim Bowers, who provided much of the financial material; and to Barbara Bentley, who contributed editorial and typing assistance through several drafts.

I also want to thank my wife, Judith, and our two sons, Edward and Arthur, from whom I have taken the time to write this book. It was not a simple task, as they can surely attest.

Brooks Fenno

Contents

1 Marketing Works!   1
2 Approaching the Selling Process   11
3 Achieving That Crucial Difference   41
4 The Art of Selling   56
5 Managing Sales Territories   75
6 Finding, Hiring, and Paying Salespeople   82
7 Getting the Most Out of Your Selling Operation   100
8 Supporting Your Selling Program Through
   Advertising   118
9 Growth by Internal Diversification   149
10 Growth by Acquisition   164
11 Funding Your Growth   189
12 Now It's Up to You!   202
   Index   217

Helping Your Business Grow

Marketing Works!

THE MARKETING CONCEPT

"If a man can write a better book, preach a better sermon, or make a better mousetrap than his neighbor, though he builds his house in the woods the world will make a beaten path to his door."

That famous pronouncement by Ralph Waldo Emerson has a nice ring, but please don't take it too seriously. I know from experience that the part about the mousetrap is dead wrong. A client of mine by the name of Martin Slutsky put time, effort, and money into a mousetrap far superior to any on the market. It electrocuted its victims and bagged the corpses for easy disposal.

Believe me, the world did not beat a path to Slutsky's door. In fact, his "better mousetrap" sold poorly. Slutsky asked me to analyze the situation. I found, for one thing, that the mousetrap was priced too high; for another, potential customers, mostly restaurants, were embarrassed to admit they had a rodent problem, even when a demonstration in their facilities produced a bag full of dead rats!

Slutsky persisted with intensive selling efforts for several years. Finally he withdrew the mousetrap from the market, a knell to a business platitude that has certainly outlived its time.

The point is, don't fall for the better mousetrap fallacy. There's more to success today than making a superior product. That's why I've written this book. I want to pass along the benefit of my experience in working with the owners of more than 100 businesses over the past 12 years. Most of my clients have sales of under $20 million. This book is for the owners of similar companies and their sales or marketing managers—anyone, that is, searching for ways to accelerate the growth of a privately held firm. My experience demonstrates that the marketing concept is not the exclusive province of larger companies. I shall show how smaller companies can use big league techniques to increase sales in efficient and profitable ways.

Throughout the book, you will find numbered "Ideas" separated from the text. These are observations, insights, maxims—call them what you will—derived from my own experience. They're meant to serve as guides and aids to marketing decisions. There are 101 ideas, covering all the significant considerations. Here's the first:

Idea #1:   The extent to which you and your firm successfully practice professional marketing will materially influence your firm's growth.

"Marketing" is a favorite business term, one that's heard every day, has been studied in business schools for years, and is enthusiastically touted by Madison Avenue. So I am often surprised to discover that otherwise knowledgeable business professionals have only the haziest notion of what marketing actually means. To some, it is just another word for sales. Nothing could be further from the truth. Marketing is a view of the entire business process as an integrated effort to identify the customer and his or her needs and to mold, promote, and distribute a product or service to fill those needs. This broad, umbrella concept covers a wide variety of policies and procedures, but marketing's fundamental goal is simple enough. It is to increase business. Here are examples of how different marketing approaches work for four of my clients.

Sorting Out Your Customers

Often regular customers offer the best opportunities for growth, especially if you know them well enough to appeal to their particular needs and desires. Take, for example, the Boston bank I worked with not long ago.

The bank had many retail customers, all of whom received the same promotions and advertisements for increased banking services. From the bank's point of view, such equal treatment didn't make much marketing sense, because one group of customers stood out from all the rest in terms of personal income. That group consisted of doctors, dentists, and other members of the medical profession. By treating this group in special ways, the bank could enhance its business opportunities substantially.

This marketing technique would have a number of advantages. For one thing, it would induce other members of the medical profession to become customers. In addition, many medical professionals require extra banking services, such as loans, to help them establish their practices. Banks, of course, make their living by loaning money. Bankers would be hard pressed to find retail borrowers more desirable than medical professionals. They represent one of the more secure investments a bank can make. Furthermore, as their income rises, they will likely turn to a bank they're familiar with for help in planning personal investments as well as for other services. So a program to seek out and attract the medical market was sure to succeed—and it did!

That is one important marketing thrust—the identification and pursuit of a special buyer segment:

Idea #2: The successful marketer continually focuses attention on buyer segments and their changing requirements.

Finding New Customers

There's no magic formula for success, but Curtis Herring discovered something mighty close to one. In 1956 he was without a job and virtually penniless. Curt formed the Gloucester Company and, with a small secondhand mixer, began making a caulking compound for the marine industry. For four years he struggled while his wife worked to support him and their children. Then, a salesman for a lumber company gave Curt an idea: Sell the caulking compound as a sealant to keep water out of the cracks in buildings. That simple idea made all the difference. Phenoseal, as the product is called, has found, on land, a whole world of new customers, and Curt is the owner of a business worth more than a million dollars.

Incidentally, the salesman who gave Curt the idea later joined him and personally sold $500,000 a year through hardware and building supply outlets before retiring. With the marine market long forgotten, the Gloucester Company now has a nationwide network of 22 sales representatives. And all this growth resulted from one critical decision—to pursue a different market.

A Five-Pronged Program

Sometimes one idea works wonders. Sometimes *five* ideas do the trick. Marketing is nothing if not varied and multifaceted. Another client, Al Hanlon, illustrates this point abundantly.

In 1967 Al bought a small display house called Admore that had sales of $90,000 and four or five employees. At the time, it was on the verge of bankruptcy. Today Admore is a highly profitable company with 25 employees and sales of $1 million a year. To achieve this growth, Al used five marketing tactics:

1. *He defined a specialized product.* Al concentrated on the design and production of trade show exhibits. He dropped ancillary products, such as point-of-sale displays, store decor designs, and industrial scale models. The idea was to be highly specialized and concentrated.

2. *He defined the market areas.* Al focused all his marketing efforts toward a clearly defined geographical area that covered all of New England, New York, and New Jersey.

3. *He expanded the service.* In Al's words: "We pioneered the idea of a trade show not as a display stand but as a method of selling and communicating an exhibitor's message to prospects. Trade show exhibits should be designed to sell the exhibitor's

merchandise. We worked out a system to do this that encompassed the training of salesmen, the preshow promotion, and the postshow audit as well as the booth design."

4. *He wrote a book.* "We were so successful," Al said, "that I wrote a book about it. My book was the first in this field and it not only enhanced my reputation but also became the backbone of our direct mail program."

5. *He analyzed accounts.* "We analyzed each category of accounts," Al said. "Why were we making money on some jobs and not on others? I began to realize that our strength was as much in the business we avoided as in the business we pursued."

I should add that Al Hanlon is a born marketer with a talent for promoting his services. Such a natural feel for marketing helps immeasurably, but it's the premise of this book that effective techniques—and especially the basic principles of marketing—can be learned and put into successful practice by all kinds of people in all kinds of businesses.

Going It Alone

Sound marketing techniques lead to growth even for one-man businesses. My client John Hofer started his own firm as a résumé writer and personnel placement advisor. He did all the work himself, including the typing.

His first marketing technique was to underprice the competition by one third. His second marketing technique was to advertise in the local newspapers and the Yellow Pages. He also promoted his service by speaking to groups of undergraduates at local community colleges. These modest efforts worked. Sales have risen by 50 percent a year for the past four years, and John has hired two full-time employees, two psychologists as contract employees, and a salesperson on commission.

He has also started to increase his marketing efforts in a number of ways:

- He monitors the cost effectiveness of his advertising by keeping a list of where and how all his new customers had heard of his service.

- He distributes a brochure addressing the major market segments that constitute his client mix.
- He conducts an aggressive selling program that includes a direct mail campaign designed to gain appointments with large firms to discuss his new outplacement service.
- He prepares personal job campaigns as a new specialized service.

With this successful experience behind him, thanks to his simple but aggressive marketing efforts, John looks forward to continued expansion. His is one business that can prosper when the economy slumps!

These four clients represent widely different aspects of the business world. Each, in his own way and on his own terms, is using marketing techniques successfully. I cite them to illustrate the variety as well as the effectiveness of the marketing approach for small businesses.

Now let's look at the other side, the common misconceptions that lead to disappointments at best, and to disasters at worst.

MARKETING MISCONCEPTIONS

It seems that every month an inventor calls on me with a product that he or she wishes to sell. Typically this inventor is an out-of-work engineer who has designed a new household gadget and has had it patented. Typically, too, the invention is not an attempt to satisfy a well-defined market requirement; instead, it's a response to a personal need of the inventor. This is one reason why less than 5 percent of all newly issued patents end up as commercially successful products (according to the recent estimates of a U.S. Department of Commerce spokesman).

As an example of how a professional marketer looks at such a new product, let's examine U.S. patent #3,861,284—"Cup Lids for the Use of Teabags and the Like." Now this product, a device for squeezing teabags, undoubtedly works and is salable. But the professional marketer asks these hard questions: Can it be sold in sufficient quantities and at an attractive enough price to make the venture worthwhile? How can tea drinkers be separated from the rest of the adult population? How are tea drinkers now squeezing teabags and with what success? Will tea drinkers invest money in a convenience item of this kind? How much?

A marketer asks such questions about any new product. They may seem obvious, but it's surprising how many products are launched before their markets are clearly understood.

Market? What Market?

This lack of understanding is not confined to naive inventors, reckless entrepreneurs, or dreamers. One of my former clients, a small tool company in Massachusetts, committed a substantial financial investment and three years of research to the development of a fully automated ribbon wire-stripping machine. It was the best and most sophisticated machine of its kind ever produced. Unfortunately, my after-the-fact research indicated that only half a dozen prospects existed nationwide for a machine of its speed and capacity. The better mousetrap fallacy claims another victim!

Even corporate giants sometimes err in their understanding of customers. General Electric and Time, Inc., both highly skilled marketers in their own areas, jointly invested $10 million to develop electronic educational materials for schools. The venture failed, mainly because school systems could not afford the sophisticated products—especially in a time of declining enrollment and growing public resistance to taxes. The failure of General Learning, as the GE/Time firm was called, stands as a cautionary legend in marketing. A seemingly unbeatable combination of money, knowledge, and talent came to naught because of insufficient attention to a basic marketing principle:

Idea #3: An effective marketer promotes a product in ways that relate to the needs of the buyer.

Here It Is! Come and Get It!

Another misconception, closely allied to the better mousetrap fallacy, is exemplified by what I call the "here it is—come and get it" approach. Actually, it is a non-approach because it ignores the needs of the buyer completely.

Take a look at the product sheet shown in Figure 1-1. It states the weight, specifications, and warranty for a portable elevating table, but that's about it. (The manufacturer's name and address have been taken off the product sheet for the purposes of this book.) "Trouble-free," "easier maneuverability," and "securely braced and reinforced" are just about the only benefits described—and they are not documented.

Figure 1-1.   Example of a product sheet.

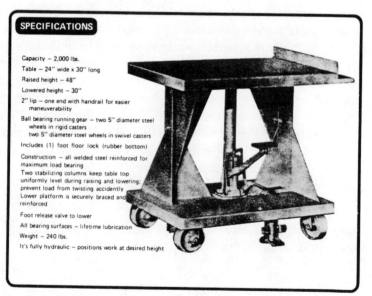

trouble-free
Portable Elevating Table

1 Year Warranty on Parts
10 Day Free Trial

SPECIFICATIONS

Capacity – 2,000 lbs.

Table – 24" wide x 30" long

Raised height – 48"

Lowered height – 30"

2" lip – one end with handrail for easier maneuverability

Ball bearing running gear – two 5" diameter steel wheels in rigid casters two 5" diameter steel wheels in swivel casters

Includes (1) foot floor lock (rubber bottom)

Construction – all welded steel reinforced for maximum load bearing

Two stabilizing columns keep table top uniformly level during raising and lowering; prevent load from twisting accidently Lower platform is securely braced and reinforced

Foot release valve to lower

All bearing surfaces – lifetime lubrication

Weight – 240 lbs.

It's fully hydraulic – positions work at desired height

Write Today . . . . . Specials on request

This product sheet represents the antithesis of good marketing practice. Where is the information that's important to the buyer? Buyers need to know what the table will do for them. They want to learn about applications, competitive advantages, equipment the table might efficiently replace—the features, in other words, that will benefit buyers. That's what marketing is all about!

The "here it is—come and get it" mistake is common among small businesses. However, it's found among large ones, too, especially high-technology companies, which promote products with litanies of hermetic technical jargon, never mentioning what the product will do for the consumer. These companies will have to relate their products to their customers' needs by using the full panoply of techniques and tactics of a sound marketing strategy. If they don't, not even their technical wizardry can save them.

A START ON STRATEGY

Every firm, large or small, must begin with a basic marketing strategy that takes into account all the ways the company's activities and products affect its customers. To begin to plan this strategy, let's consider the separate elements of marketing. They are:

1. Market research and planning.
   - Defining who the buyer is, what he or she wants and is willing to pay for, and how much he or she will pay.
   - Determining how to give customers what they want most efficiently and profitably.
2. Product or service development.
   - Shaping it to meet the predefined need.
   - Packaging and labeling it effectively.
   - Devising in-store promotion to enhance sales.
   - Pricing competitively at all levels: base price, point of shipment, commissions, discounts.
3. Distribution.
   - Moving the product or service efficiently to a location where customers will buy it.
   - Presenting it effectively.

4. Advertising.
   - Developing sales leads.
   - Using public relations and advertising to promote a favorable image.

5. Sales.
   - Direct (through factory salesperson).
   - Indirect (through sales representatives or distributor salespersons).
   - Sales support (by telephone or mail by employees inside manufacturer's office).

6. Post-sale follow-up.
   - Timeliness of delivery.
   - Technical service.
   - Sales and profit analysis.

We will take a close look at these elements in subsequent chapters. They comprise the "marketing mix," the ingredients of your strategy. The important point to note at this stage is that the elements are closely interrelated. That's what marketing as a concept is all about. It's not a trick or a gimmick or a set of ploys. It's a comprehensive approach that relates your business and your product or service to buyers in many different ways, all of which are geared to work in harmony. In its intricacy and scope, marketing is a fascinating study. Psychology, finance, demographics, technology enter into it—you can make it as complex as you like! But, in beginning to think about your marketing strategy, keep in mind one important fact: The buyer is the key to the whole process.

So let's start with the shadowy, anonymous figure of the buyer and see what the tools of market research can help us learn about him or her.

CHAPTER 2

Approaching the Selling Process

MARKET RESEARCH—THE KEY TO EFFECTIVE SELLING

Research constitutes a key element in any marketing program and often makes the difference between success and failure. Yet many businessmen, impatient to get going, neglect research because it takes too long, requires skills and knowledge they don't possess, and is too expensive. That's a mistake.

Who Is Your Customer?

Market research simply means finding out as much as possible about your customers and potential customers in order to serve them effectively. The information such research provides is essential to sound marketing decisions, so it's well worth the time it takes. Its basic tools, as we shall see in this chapter, are readily available, easy to use, and not at all expensive.

Idea #4: The starting point in marketing is the identification of the real buyer or target marketing group.

11

This is what market research is all about. It consists of applying established techniques to the process of identifying who your customers are, what their needs and buying habits are, what their response to your product is, and why they buy your product instead of your competitors'. *Don't guess. Find out.* That's the marketer's credo. And it applies to both consumer and industrial markets. Let's look at the consumer field first.

Not long ago, I had a client who saw an opportunity to start a new business in Boston. He was familiar with the food delivery business in the city, and he knew that most firms in this field depended almost entirely on word-of-mouth advertising and on displays in the Yellow Pages. He also knew that they sold a product of unknown quantity and quality under a complex and often confusing price structure. In other words, their approach to customers was essentially passive.

My client founded Mister Party, Inc., a catering service designed to beat its competition by using an aggressive and straightforward marketing approach. His fundamental assumption was that customers would appreciate knowing what the menu would be and how much it would cost—before they made a purchase. He also believed that customers would respond favorably to an attractive, easy-to-open package that contained all the required accessories (tablecloth, napkins, utensils, and so on). When the meal was finished, the dishes and remnants could be collected, placed back in the original container, and easily discarded.

In addition to this attractive package, my client listed the dishes available in a handsome brochure, with color photos appetizingly depicting his menus. He priced each menu on a per-person basis so that the purchaser could quickly determine the total cost. He charged extra only for door-to-door delivery.

He was all set. But as his marketing consultant, I advised that he take a good hard look at his potential audience before going ahead. Who, precisely, would be interested in his unique service? Through research, we attempted to answer the following questions:

- Should Mister Party try to reach the home party giver?
- What income group would be receptive to this service? For what kind of function?

- Would married people be the prime target, or do they tend to prefer preparing their own dishes?
- How about single party throwers? Are they numerous enough and affluent enough to seek the services of a caterer?
- What about the industrial market? Would a company called Mister Party, Inc., appeal to business executives and lawyers, for example, who didn't have time to go out for lunch but wanted more than the usual sandwich fare for themselves and their clients?

Beyond the answers to such basic questions, my client needed to know under what circumstances people decide to buy a catered product. Do they order out at the last minute, when it becomes clear they haven't enough time to prepare the food themselves? When they're at the package store buying liquor, do they think, "I better get some food, too—or my guests will get soused?"

We were all confident that Mister Party was a good idea, and that my client had the knowledge and experience to carry it off successfully. Yet the hard questions had to be asked. The answers provided a solid groundwork for a successful business. Market research gave us a precise identification of our target audience early on. That saved an incalculable amount of time, effort, and money. It may well have provided the client with the information he needed to pinpoint his services to precisely the right market: social gatherings and middle-income party goers.

Idea #5:   To be successful, you, the marketer, must know not only who the buyers are but how they buy—what their consumer behavior is.

The history of another client underscores this point. The client is a manufacturer of plastic signs who had designed a U-shaped tennis ball holder that snapped onto a player's tennis dress or shorts and held the server's second ball. The tennis ball holder worked very well, and its inventor gave an effective demonstration of its capabilities before a large audience at the Boston Tennis

Center. Surprisingly, there were no follow-up orders. The demonstration was a great success, but it didn't sell any ball holders.

So the inventor came to me for marketing guidance. After a preliminary study it was obvious that the buyer for the ball holder was female. A man has a pocket in his shorts designed to hold the second ball, and a man's hands are usually large enough to hold two balls at once, should he prefer. Thus, the market was clearly defined and the market need identified.

Further market research revealed, however, that women's vanity outweighed their need for the ball holder—they simply were not willing to accept the bulge that distorted the fashionable lines of a dress. That product didn't have a chance! Market research of a very basic and simple kind saved the inventor a substantial investment in a product doomed to failure.

As you can see, market research provides businesspeople with a sound, scientific attitude toward their markets as well as a methodology for asking the right questions. The attitude is just as important as the methodology. Don't rely on instinct or hunches alone, the marketer says. Ask the hard questions. Don't move ahead with a new product or try to enter a new market for an established product until you have precise information about its buyers.

How do you define the buyer and learn about his or her methods of consumption? Here are the main kinds of information you need to seek out:

1. Personal characteristics:
   - Age.
   - Sex.
   - Ethnic and religious background.
   - Social class.
   - Occupation and position.
   - Family relationships (married, single, divorced).
   - Geographical location (country, region, state, county and town).

2. Income characteristics:
   - Total income.
   - Disposable income.

3. Consumer behavior:
   - Spending habits (rate and methods of expenditures, benefits sought, criteria for evaluating alternatives).
   - Savings patterns.

Sources of Information

Published Information

The U.S. Bureau of Census is the most frequently used statistical source of information about economic and personal characteristics of the population. The figures appear in a book titled *Characteristics of the Population*, published by the U.S. Department of Commerce in a series of volumes, one for each state. Most libraries have the entire series, so it is available to you free of charge. The same data, in perhaps more readable and useful form, may also be obtained from private research firms, which charge a fee for their service. The information in *Characteristics of the Population* is based on the census taken at the beginning of each decade and is published every 10 years. Figures are broken out by state, county, town, and standard metropolitan statistical areas (SMSAs) for a large number of personal and income characteristics.

Consumer Research Services

For information tailored specifically to your business, there are many consumer market research services available from a wide range of local and national firms. Most are listed in *International Directory of Marketing Research Houses and Services*, published annually by the New York Chapter of the American Marketing Association. Look in the Yellow Pages of your phone book for those serving your area. These companies will gather data for you by having interviewers telephone home dwellers during the day or evening or by interviewing shoppers at, typically, a shopping mall. Most market research firms tend to avoid using direct mail surveys or door-to-door personal interviews. The mail surveys usually get too low a rate of response for statistical accuracy (unless an expensive premium is offered as an inducement to the respondee). Door-to-door interviews are almost always more expensive than they are worth. For one thing, with so many working wives these days, interviewers don't find many consumers at home.

Consumer Sampling: The Critical Factors

Obviously, the best way to find out about your customers is to hear from them directly. Professional market research firms can be of inestimable help in identifying your customers. Don't forget, though, that the reliability of the information they collect depends on many factors. Market researchers are usually careful to advise you about the potential pitfalls inherent in all sampling techniques, but you should be aware of three factors affecting the reliability of the information you receive:

1. *Correct interpretation of the questions.* Remember, your questions must be understood first by the data collection agency, then by the interviewer, and finally by the person being interviewed. The questionnaire is not always as self-explanatory as you think it is. The responses then have to be categorized to provide a simple and meaningful conclusion.

2. *Representativeness of the sample.* The group sampled must mirror the group you want to find out about, but there are two major reasons why that isn't always the case. First, it is easy to err in judgments about who is truly representative. If you assume, for example, that the man in a household is the decision maker in buying a second automobile, you may well be wrong. Often, the woman makes that selection.

Second, your research firm may inadvertently interview the wrong people. A classic example was the *Literary Digest* opinion poll in 1936, which picked Landon to beat Roosevelt for the U.S. presidency. Roosevelt overwhelmingly defeated Landon, receiving 523 out of a possible 531 electoral votes. The *Literary Digest* sent out 10 million straw ballots and received 2,376,523 replies—an excellent response, and one presumably large enough for a statistically valid projection. The key mistake lay in the fact that the mailing list was compiled from telephone directories and automobile registration files. It was well suited for the *Digest's* commercial purposes of sales promotions for potential subscribers, but it was not a representative cross section of the U.S. voting population in 1936.

3. *Size of sample.* In general, the reliability of statistical data increases as the size of the sample on which it is based increases. As a rule of thumb,* where a statistic is expressed in the form of a percentage, the odds are nine out of ten that:

If the sample size is approximately:	*The statistic is reliable within the limits of approximately:*
25	+ or − 16.5%
50	+ or − 11.7%
75	+ or − 9.5%
100	+ or − 8.3%
200	+ or − 5.8%
300	+ or − 4.8%
500	+ or − 3.7%
800	+ or − 2.9%
1,000	+ or − 2.6%

According to the above chart, if 25 percent of the people in your sample say they buy your product, and the random sample size is 100 people, the chances are nine out of ten that the true figure for the entire population lies between 16.7 percent and 33.3 percent (25% ± 8.3%). Although a larger sample yields more accurate data, it makes for a much more expensive research project. Therefore, the size of the sample should be determined by weighing the need for accuracy against the money available.

Focus Groups

For existing products, one effective way of getting information about consumer preferences, purchasing habits, and attitudes is through what market researchers call "focus groups." A trained group leader conducts a discussion with 6 to 12 consumers for an

* From a privately published monograph by Richard Manville, "Steps in Conducting a Marketing Research Study," Westport, CT, 1966.

hour or two. The leader asks questions and directs the conversation toward answers of value to his client.

Suppose, for instance, that your product is an electric can opener. The group leader would have your product and all your major competitors' products on hand and would ask the group to look them over. The leader would ask group members about their preferences. "Do you use this kind of appliance every day?" "What are the qualities that you like about can openers? What do you dislike?" "Do you prefer one brand name over another?" And so on. This kind of discussion yields much in-depth information about your customers' preferences, purchasing habits, and other considerations. Often, you as sponsor can view the proceedings through a one-way window that allows you to monitor the verbal interplay between the participants without being seen. The identity of the focus group's sponsor is often concealed from the group at the beginning of the discussion, when participants compare the various products available. Otherwise, the results are to be viewed with skepticism. People tend to tell you what they think you want to hear.

There are many marketing research groups that stage focus groups. They provide the setting, select the participants, and report their findings. Look in the Yellow Pages under "Marketing Research," or consult the *International Directory of Marketing Research Houses and Services.*

When properly conducted, focus groups provide valuable insights into customer attitudes and preferences, but the data from one or several such meetings should not be taken at face value. A few small meetings may or may not be representative of your overall market.

The Basic Questions of Market Research

Whether your research into consumer buying habits is elaborate or simple, whether you spend much money or little, whether you hire consultants or do it yourself, the end result is the answer to questions in five key areas about your customers and their buying patterns. The U.S. Army calls these basic questions "the keys to information." Every novice news reporter learns them as a way of thinking about a story. They are: Who? What? When? Where? How?

Answers to these questions will usually give you an accurate picture of a selected market:

- *Who* makes the buying decision? Who influences the buying decision? Who purchases the product or service? Who uses it?
- *What* is the current need? What products or services are now being used to meet that need? What problems are being encountered by the consumer? What are the purchasing patterns of the consumer?
- *When* is the product or service bought? Is it seasonal?
- *Where* is the buying decision made—at home or at the point of purchase? Where is the purchase made?
- *How* does the customer now buy the product? How does he or she wish to buy it? How is the product used? How does the customer purchase the product again? How is the product financed and serviced?

Market research agencies and consultants can prepare and conduct consumer surveys that will help answer those basic questions. Professionals understand the quirks and pitfalls of all polling techniques, and they know how to use consumer research to help you plan for larger sales and increased business.

However, you may prefer to do your own market research by preparing your own questionnaires and conducting your own surveys. If so, keep in mind the following advice:

Idea #6: Structure the questionnaire to facilitate easy tabulation of results.

Idea #7: Always pretest opinion questionnaires. Try them out on volunteers, using the planned interviewing procedures.

Industrial Market Research

For good reasons, most market research focuses on the consumer, rather than the industrial, market. The consumer market is large and complex, and marketers of consumer products are more sophisticated in marketing techniques than their industrial counterparts. Still, industrial market research can play an important part in selling your products to other firms. Many consumer products are needed and bought in quantity by larger firms, so it is worth your time and effort to explore the industrial market as fully as possible. Most industrial market research is conducted by large companies for their own use, and the information is not available to small firms. However, large trade associations usually employ market analysts whose work is available to all members. In addition, there is much information available to all companies, large and small, from many other sources.

Sources of Industrial Market Information

Idea #8:   The best and often least used source of industrial market data can be found in a company's own customer files.

Don't overlook all the information gathered over the years about your customers. Historical data immediately available in your own files can provide the best description of future prospects of any that you may get outside. If you're looking for ways to expand, a sound first step would be to do some research in your own organization. You may find a gold mine of prospects in your records of former customers—a good place to start in looking for new leads.

In addition, remember that your current customer lists provide a profile of the kind of customers you are most likely to find. The lists give you a microcosm of the marketplace in terms of the services they provide, their size, geographical location, and the types of companies that signal your best opportunities. And don't stop there. Other in-company sources worth continuing analysis are salespersons' reports and records, salespersons' reports on lost sales, and prospect lists.

When you've thoroughly searched company records, it's time to turn to outside sources. Here are the principal sources of information about industrial prospects:

• *Trade and professional association surveys.* Many trade associations maintain statistics on their industries. *The National Trade and Professional Associations of the United States and Canada & Labor Unions* is a publication available at many business libraries. It can be purchased for $30 from Room 601, 734 Fifteenth Street, Washington, D.C. 20005. Another basic source book is *The Encyclopedia of Associations,* which lists all industrial associations alphabetically by type of industry. It's available in most business libraries.

• *Business and trade journals and periodicals.* A selection of the more important articles are indexed in the *Business Periodicals Index* (BPI). A new BPI is published monthly. It contains a wealth of material on nearly every subject relevant to business. The title of each article is referenced to the periodical in which it appeared. Recent volumes of the BPI are available in business libraries and in many public libraries. A good guide to business and trade publications is *The Standard Periodical Directory,* readily available in all libraries.

Many trade and business publications produce an annual statistical issue devoted to their specialties. Look for the issues in areas that may be potential markets for your company. In digging out this kind of statistical information, don't forget that it's perfectly O.K. to call the editor of a trade or business publication and ask for additional statistics and tips on other sources of information about a particular company or industry. Predicasts, Inc., issues a quarterly publication that projects future sales for a broad range of industries. These projections are based on data taken from trade publications within each industry. *Predicasts* can be found in many business libraries.

• *U.S. Government.* The Department of Commerce produces the *Guide to Industrial Statistics,* which lists all the government publications containing data about industry. These include the

Census of Manufacturers, published every five years (one appears in 1982) in four volumes. The Census of Manufacturers lists firms by size, geographic location, and type of product. Its four volumes cover the subject matter in this way:

Volume I—Summary Statistics.
Volume II—Industry Statistics. This volume delineates all businesses by product classification.
Volume III—Area Series. This volume delineates businesses by geographic (state, county, and SMSA).
Volume IV—Indexes of Production.

The Department of Commerce also publishes two other volumes of value to industrial market researchers. One is the Annual Survey of Manufacturers which gives statistics by industries, industry groups and geographic areas. It is published as an abbreviated trend supplement to the Census of Manufacturers to provide some census statistics in non-census years. The other is County Business Patterns, which provides an excellent and detailed numerical breakout of businesses by type, size, and county within each state.

The Departments of Labor and Agriculture and the Small Business Administration also produce a variety of publications of use to an industrial market researcher. Information about what's available can be obtained by contacting the separate publications offices.

Directories. There are regional and state business directories covering every part of the United States. They list all major manufacturing and service firms, giving address, phone number, type of business, and size, and are very valuable sales prospecting references. George D. Hall publishes the Directory of New England Manufacturers, in addition to similar books listing companies in many other states. The major business directories are:

- Dun & Bradstreet's Million Dollar Directory (three volumes). The first volume lists U.S. firms with a net worth of $1 million or more. The second volume lists firms with a net worth of $500,000 to $999,999. The third volume lists firms with a net worth of less than $500,000. Many privately owned firms are included in these listings. All companies are listed both alphabetically and by type of product.

- Moody's *Industrial Manual* presents financial data taken from the balance sheets of major publically held industrial firms.
- *Thomas Register.* This is a commercial publication that lists all manufacturing firms in the United States. It is frequently used by company purchasing agents to identify new sources of supply. The *Thomas Register* comes in 16 volumes. Volumes 1 through 8 break down specific manufacturers by size within product categories and subdivides locations by city and town. Volumes 9 and 10 give the names, addresses, and telephone numbers of all listed firms. Volumes 11 to 16 contain catalog sheets submitted by manufacturers.
- *Directory of U.S. and Canadian Marketing Surveys Services* gives 2,150 market research reports, each privately compiled and available for a fee of from several hundred to a thousand dollars.
- *Findex* contains 2,500 market research reports and surveys conducted in the United States and is similar to the *Directory of U.S. and Canadian Marketing Surveys Services.*
- *The Directory of Directories* lists more than 5,000 directories, many of which give regional and state information pertaining to companies that may be sales prospects for your firm.

The SIC Code: Your Most Important Aid

Of all the sources for industrial market research none is more useful than the Standard Industrial Classification system, called SIC for short. This system has been prepared by the U.S. Bureau of the Budget and is fully explained and documented in the *Standard Industrial Classification Manual.* The value of SIC is that every company, including yours and mine, is represented in at least one category and can be readily identified in terms of its product, number of employees, and location. The SIC has many uses, perhaps the most important of which is in the development of sales leads, so we'll save a discussion of its specific applications for Chapter 8, "Supporting Your Selling Program Through Advertising."

Cutting Through the Research Morass

The sources given above constitute the primary tools of industrial market research, but there are new tools available that can save you a lot of legwork. Hundreds of computerized data sources have emerged in recent years, and they can often deliver the information you need with speed and accuracy. It's always good to keep in mind, however, that these sources are only as good as the data base they access. Garbage in, garbage out, as the computer freaks say. Ask your business librarian about bibliographical search services that are now widely available for a reasonable fee.

As a result of the information explosion, a number of data source brokerage firms have been founded across the country. For a fee, these firms will help you search for industrial market information of any kind. Warner-Eddison Associates offers these services in the Boston area, and Find/SVP is one of the leading information brokerages in New York. On the West Coast, there's Information On Demand, located in Berkeley, California. Many other such organizations are listed in the membership directory of the Information Industry Association. For a copy, write: Information Industry Association, Suite 904, 4720 Montgomery Lane, Bethesda, MD 20014.

THE NEXT STEP: PLANNING YOUR PROGRAM

Market research is only the first important step in approaching the selling process. There's another important step, a preliminary to successful selling, and that entails planning a course of action. "Plan your work, and work your plan." This maxim can't be ignored when developing an effective program.

The Need for a Goal

"Would you tell me, please, which way I ought to walk from here?" said Alice to the cat.

"That depends a good deal on where you want to get to," said the cat.

"I don't much care where," said Alice.

"Then it doesn't matter which way you walk," said the cat.

That snatch of dialogue from *Alice in Wonderland* contains a profound truth for all businessmen.

Idea #9: If you don't know where you are going, any path will get you there.

This simple axiom was first brought to my attention by Ray Chartier, president of Standard Duplicator Sales, a Boston office equipment dealer. He had heard it from a professor at the Harvard Business School. I pass it along to my clients at every opportunity, because I firmly believe it represents a key to success in business.

Idea #10: Only by setting well-defined objectives can you make decisions logically and efficiently—and thereby maximize your firm's growth potential.

Small businessmen are often entrepreneurs who like the free-wheeling, seat-of-the-pants aspect of their work. Many who have brought their business to a size that assures continued survival (roughly a net worth of at least $1 million) are content to watch the company's growth ebb and flow with the regional economic tide. In good times, they and their marketing managers are too busy filling orders to worry about planning for accelerated future growth. In a slack economy, they have the time but are too concerned about conserving funds to pursue new growth ideas.

This is an understandable pattern, but not a desirable one. I have seen any number of business people who could have slipped into an "any road will take you there" frame of mind, but didn't. Instead, they took a good hard look at their business, employed the techniques of market research to identify new potential customers, and then set up clear goals that they and their staffs went to work on and achieved.

What Your Game Plan Will Do for You

Your game plan not only aids in decision making by providing a frame of reference, but it helps in two other important areas as well. First, it furnishes an overall direction for your company. This direction in marketing may result in your company targeting a certain pre-determined market segment or mix of segments for pursuit. As an example, consider The Boston Envelope Company, an independent manufacturer of envelopes with annual sales of over $10 million. Boston Envelope has succeeded because it had a very precise plan for concentrating on the medium-run envelope market (250,000 to 1,000,000 envelopes per order) and on specialty envelopes within the Northeastern region. If Boston Envelope had not defined this market precisely and pursued it with vigor, the chances are that its sales efforts would have been scattered and ineffective. Pinpoint planning has been the key to its success.

Second, a game plan fosters an efficient corporate structure because it provides clearly understood direction. Such a structure facilitates the selection of the proper type and number of people and the assignment of meaningful jobs. In Boston Envelope's case, by knowing the market segment it wishes to pursue, management is able to determine the number and type of prospects within that segment. This permits the owners to determine how many outside and inside salespeople they need (and can afford), what the goals of these salespeople should be, and what sort of advertising support they should receive.

Many owners complain that they'd love to have the time to develop a business plan, but it's impossible because of the day-to-day press of business. I understand their problem, but I believe that any owner who wants a business to grow can find the time. And it's not that hard; the information and thinking that goes into an ordinary working day provides much of the groundwork for a solid game plan. You simply have to crystallize those hazy ideas about future prospects into a clear, objective form that draws on what you know about your company and what you've learned through experience and market research about your customers. Some owners of very small businesses really are too busy (or too harried) to come up with a good game plan. But once a manufacturer or a service company grosses over $1 million in annual sales (or a distributor over $3 million) the owner must make the time to plan—even if it means adding staff to lighten the day-to-day workload.

Idea #11:   Upon reaching sales in excess of $1 million an owner should set aside half a day a week for exposure to new concepts (through seminars, workshops, and so on) and for planning.

Once past this "survival threshhold" the owner shouldn't have to worry about daily problems and shouldn't have to plug holes in the dike to keep the operation going. That's the time to look around and see what's happening inside and outside the industry—and to set and achieve goals. For some it's a difficult transition, but for ambitious owners who can manage competently and set goals effectively, the game is surely worth the candle.

Idea #12:   A business owner can usually buy the talent to translate goals into reality, but the goals themselves must come from the owner.

How to Shape Your Game Plan

Once a problem has been properly defined the solution often becomes obvious. Similarly, the ways to achieve goals often become apparent once the goals have been set. Consider, for instance, a company that has been growing at a rate of 10 to 15 percent a year. If the president seeks a sales increase of 15 percent for the next year, all that is required is that he do what he has been doing a little better, and throw in a price increase. But if that president seeks a 50 percent sales increase, he must alter his current method of operation because he needs to generate an additional 35 percent in sales over and above his normal growth rate. The president could attempt to achieve this goal in several ways: by altering his current marketing program (adding salespeople, increasing pro-

motional activities, and so on), pursuing new markets, or introducing a new product or service.

Of course, most presidents aren't that ambitious or that optimistic about rapid growth. Here is a model of a more modest
game plan showing the projected sales revenues of XYZ Company:

Item	Resulting Sales
Maintaining current sales level	$1.5 million
A normal growth, including inflationary price increases	.2 million
Adding a third outside salesperson	.5 million
Doubling advertising budget to obtain a 50 percent increase in sales leads	.2 million
Entering a second trade show	.2 million

Good game plans come in all shapes and sizes, depending on
the business and the personalities of the owner and the sales
manager. Many successful small business owners would be aghast
at the time and detail that goes into preparing an annual budget
for Procter & Gamble, for instance. However, it's not the form but
the critical analysis of the business that counts—the quality of
thought, in other words.

Annual Sales Forecast

In marketing, the annual sales forecast is the most common
type of game plan. It is usually prepared one to three months
before the beginning of the new fiscal year. Typically, this forecast
is submitted in draft form to the owner or marketing manager by
the sales manager, who bases its content on a review of past sales
figures and on discussions with the sales staff. Such discussions
should include a consideration of all major prospects, with projected dollars sales adjusted for the probability of occurrence. In
developing a forecast the sales manager should combine the figures for each salesperson's territory. A typical projection might
look like the one in Figure 2-1.

Figure 2-1. Sample sales projection.

	Salesperson **A**	Territory Forecast	
	Major prospects for achieving 1983 sales projection		
Prospects	Anticipated Sales	× Probability of Closing	= Weighted Estimate
Current prospects			
Siegfried Co.	$160,000	.75	$120,000
Acme Paints	80,000	.50	40,000
Ryan Brothers	110,000	.50	55,000
Batel Fabricators	80,000	.25	20,000
Repeat business	294,000	.90	465,000
			$700,000
New Prospects			500,000
Total forecast for 1983			$1,200,000

Once the sales manager has submitted his draft, the owner should "negotiate" a target forecast that is acceptable to both parties. For their own protection, sales managers should be conservative in their sales projections, but most are overly optimistic about expressing what they can produce.

Most sales projections are quite simple in construction. For example, take a look at Figure 2-2, which shows the projections of the lumber company. The owner and sales manager jointly

Figure 2-2. The 1983 sales forecast of a lumber company.

Yard	1982 Actual Sales (000)	1983 Forecast Sales (000)	Difference
Boston	$ 975.0	$1072.0	$ 97.0
Roslindale	875.0	970.0	95.0
Randolph	500.0	548.0	48.0
Westwood	285.0	313.5	28.5
Norwell	0	455.0	455.0
	$2635.0	$3358.5	$723.5 (+27%)

projected sales to industrial institutional and municipal accounts for their five lumber yards.

As a next step the sales forecast should be translated into the budget. Be aware that the two are *not* the same.

Idea #13: In preparing a realistic budget projection, the owner of a company should reduce the announced unit sales by 5 to 15 percent to accommodate unforeseen problems and to offset the optimism of the sales manager.

The Long-Range Plan

The long-range plan is more a strategy tool than a vehicle of immediate utility. Large companies often update their long-range plan annually. Some will have a fixed year for completion, but most slide the plan ahead five years from each review date. It is not particularly important which route the small business owner takes—just having a plan is enough! However, the plan should be expressed in writing in order to crystallize the document and the thoughts of the owner.

Your long-range plans should be set down as clearly and specifically as possible. Figure 2-3 shows an excellent model from one of my clients, Spectra-Polymer, Inc., of Ashburnham, Massachusetts.

A practical approach is to prepare an annual report for your board of directors each year. The board can be a "working" board of directors, a legal board (to comply with the incorporation statement of your company; usually consists of family members), or simply certain selected individuals. Since my firm is not incorporated, I prepare my annual report for myself and my family because I profit greatly from the thought and input that the task requires. Figure 2-4 shows how I set it up.

Monitoring Sales Progress

The critical elements for your plans and programs for growth are the numerical objectives (sales and profits) and how well you achieve them. One way of monitoring sales progress is to establish

Figure 2-3.   Sample long-range plan. (Courtesy Spectra-Polymer, Inc.)

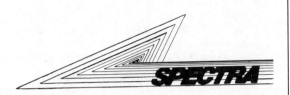

Spectra Polymer, Inc. is a specialty plastic additives manufacturer. Our products are dry colors, color concentrates, and plastic compounds. These materials are used by other manufacturers who injection-mold, blow-mold, or extrude thermoplastic resins.

The plastics industry has been growing at a rate of 12% per year over the last ten years. Within the plastics industry, color concentrates continue to grow at a rate close to 20% per year.

Resin production totaled 35.3 billion lbs. in 1979, according to data from the Society of Plastics Industry Committee on Resin Statistics. This output exceeds the 1978 level by 10.9%.

Predicasts, Inc., the Cleveland-based research firm, reports that thermoplastics will continue to be the fastest-growing materials used in the United States throughout the 1980s. The annual growth is expected to be in excess of 8% and push consumption of thermoplastics past the 75-billion-pound mark.

Spectra Polymer, Inc. currently sells over a million dollars' worth of products and services per year to approximately 150 accounts, mainly in the New England area. Sales have increased from $631,000 in 1977 to $912,000 in 1979. During this period we instituted financial controls: budgets, cost accounting, monthly receivable and payable agings, monthly cash flow statements, and periodic forecasts. Our goals for the next five years are:

	1981	1982	1983	1984	1985
Sales	$1,485,000	2,000,000	2,500,000	3,000,000	3,500,000
Profits	$ 48,300	70,000	93,750	120,000	149,800

The direction Spectra Polymer, Inc. will take to reach these goals will be:

1. Build a sales organization to expand coverage in New England and upper New York state.
2. Expand concentrate capability to all "engineering resins."
3. Expand concentrate capability in "universal concentrates."
4. Separate compounding operation, and use the resources toward the concentrates.

5. Build new facilities to increase efficiency.
6. Initiate an around-the-clock production and lab operation for maximum output and efficiency.
7. Maintain an R&D program to develop new products and new markets for existing products.
8. Increase return on investment from 10% to 15%.

To reach these five-year goals, Spectra Polymer will use this strategy:

A. Sales Area

1. Increase our sales force to 3 salespeople for New England and upper New York state plus three manufacturers' representatives by 1985.
2. Expand in our present market areas, that is, injection molders, blow molders, and sheet and profile extrusion, particularly the 5000-lb.-and-under market.
3. Expand dry colors in VHMWPE and rotational molding markets.
4. Increase the use of the telephone for sales follow-up.
5. Put emphasis on service. Strong backup needed from the laboratory and five-day delivery needed from production.
6. Conduct market research and make sales calls on all "engineering resin" users.
7. Study customer potential for "universal color" applications.
8. Price competitively in areas where we seek greater market penetration. Strong backup needed from the lab to develop less expensive formulas, from the purchasing department for savings, and from production for greater efficiency.
9. Design and implement printing of new logo on all stationery and packaging items to dress up image.
10. Establish advertising budget. Make up new brochure with color chips. Send out bulletins on new developments by direct mailing. Consider entering trade shows by 1983.
11. Install computer and necessary software for sales control of salespeople and for marketing information.

B. Production

1. Design efficient plant for materials flow and cleanliness. Meet OSHA and EPA requirements.
2. Upgrade equipment for greater output, energy conservation, and less downtime.

3. Perfect systems and procedures for increased efficiency and better quality.
4. Train personnel in these systems and write procedure manuals.
5. Devise incentives to keep personnel.
6. Initiate chart system for regular preventative maintenance check for each piece of equipment.
7. Make capital investment needed to reach goals and to give top-quality service to customers.
8. Plan for and initiate an around-the-clock operation.

C. Laboratory

1. Initiate R&D to develop new products, exploit new market, and improve quality.
2. Find new markets for existing technology (i.e. dry colors for rotational molding and ultra-high molecular weight polyethylene).
3. Test and add new pigments and resins that increase our advantage over competitors.
4. Develop stock colors for some resins and for color chip book used by customers sharing these colors.
5. Improve laboratory facilities and equipment for increased output, more efficiency, and better quality control.
6. Plan and initiate an around-the-clock operation. Hire and train three technicians, two colorists, and a new technical director.

D. Finance

1. Improve cash position and keep good cash flow during difficult growth period by keeping current cash flow statements and anticipating cash requirements.
2. Keep inventory down. Increase turnover rate to six times per year.
3. Plan for inventory to be lowest at the end of June and December, when crucial financial statements come out. If this is not possible, consider changing fiscal year.
4. Keep tight budget controls and feedback.
5. Improve return on investment from present 10% to 15% by 1985. This may not be possible for the next two years after the large capital investment until the profits picture improves from higher sales and greater utilization of assets.
6. Install computer, necessary software, and operator to aid implementation of financial and inventory controls.

Management's Forecast for the Next Five Years

Inflation will undoubtedly continue unchecked, averaging 10% per year over the next five years. There will probably be an expanding economy alternating with a contracting economy as the government tries to control inflation. We must try to expand as much as possible when the economy is rising and try to hold our own during contraction, while getting in position for the next rise. Material prices and labor costs will be going up, making it difficult to keep up with pricing. We must keep current in order to stay profitable. Our customers will also be having the same problems with inflation and will be looking for ways to cut costs. Gasoline prices will be rising—there may also be shortages—and this will make traveling and sales costs per call more expensive. New, imaginative sales techniques and more selective sales calls will be necessary.

Competition will be stronger. Larger companies with greater resources will continue to buy out the smaller color companies, pulling together a fragmented business. However, because we are in a service business for injection molders, blow molders, and sheet extruders, volume production and pricing will not be as effective as in volume markets, such as the film industry. There are a dozen color companies in New England alone, making it a particularly competitive area. The New York City and New Jersey areas are also heavy with concentrate manufacturers that spread out into New England. We must keep costs under control to price competitively, and we must also maintain an adequate production capacity in order to give better service than competition.

Regulation at the federal and state levels will continue. The next big push will be to control dumping of hazardous chemicals. There may be a slowing down of new regulation by OSHA, but no pullback of present regulation. Our customers will be nervous. A strong, knowledgeable stance will be required. Close contact with our customers to determine their exact requirements and end uses will keep our customers out of trouble, win goodwill, and bring us orders.

One of the big economic influences of the next five years will be the "reindustrialization" climate to increase productivity. The rumblings are found at the federal level and state level (with the "Make it in Massachusetts" slogan). There will be more incentives for expansion for Spectra and for our customers. Electronics will be especially strong in New England, so more engineering resins will be needed. This atmosphere should encourage new technology in new resins and new equipment. It will also mean new products by our customers. New important colors are unlikely, but as prices of so-called inexpensive pigments move up, better value will be found in some of the higher-priced colors. Altogether, the next five years could be the most expansive since the sixties.

CASH FLOW STATEMENT

	1981	1982	1983	1984	1985
Receipts					
Dry Colors	135,000	150,000	175,000	190,000	200,000
Concentrates	1,350,000	1,850,000	2,325,000	2,810,000	3,300,000
Compounding	—	—	—	—	—
Total Receipts	1,485,000	2,000,000	2,500,000	3,000,000	3,500,000
Disbursements					
Purchases—Raw Materials	816,750	1,100,000	1,375,000	1,650,000	1,925,000
Payroll—Gross Pay	292,408	386,269	488,621	609,588	710,978
Payroll—FICA and State Tax	25,149	34,078	42,346	51,712	59,169
Payroll—Insurance	43,938	50,528	58,107	63,918	70,309
Payroll—Uniforms	5,750	6,690	8,280	11,040	11,995
Rent and Lease	15,109	15,109	15,109	15,109	7,554
Property and Business Tax	—	30,000	30,000	30,000	30,000
Repairs and Maintenance	31,700	31,800	33,000	36,300	39,930
Advertising	10,000	10,000	15,000	25,000	35,000
Automobile	8,954	12,368	20,273	22,300	24,530
Delivery	10,034	13,290	16,413	17,413	20,025
Dues and Licenses	—	—	—	—	—
Insurance	4,500	4,500	4,500	4,500	4,500
Interest	72,822	82,150	76,851	68,650	70,722
Legal and Audit	3,000	3,300	3,600	4,000	4,400
Supplies—Office and Mfg.	29,055	36,400	44,550	49,005	53,905
Telephone	8,465	10,000	12,500	17,500	19,250
Travel	12,000	20,000	29,700	31,900	38,060
Utilities	39,634	46,791	54,950	64,633	71,096
Other	6,389	6,700	7,375	8,107	8,500
Total Disbursements	1,435,657	1,899,976	2,336,175	2,780,675	3,204,824
Cash					
Cash from Operations	49,343	100,024	163,825	219,325	295,176
Cash—Start of Period	11,000	152,601	205,737	319,535	452,362
Total Cash	60,343	252,625	369,562	538,860	747,538
Other Payments					
Asset Purchases	600,000	190,000	151,000	35,000	13,000
Loan Repayment	72,742	45,888	50,027	86,498	87,416
Equity Withdrawals	—	—	—	—	—
Total Other Payments	672,742	235,888	201,027	121,498	100,416
Other Receipts					
Sale of Assets	165,000	—	—	—	—
Bank Loan	600,000	190,000	151,000	35,000	—
Total Other Receipts	765,000	190,000	151,000	35,000	—
Cash—End of Period (total cash minus payments plus receipts)	152,601	206,737	319,535	452,362	647,122

Figure 2-4.   Format used for SALESMARK's annual report.

Accomplishments for the past year

    Financial figures: Sales _____   Profit _____

    Performance:

        Number of customers served _____

        Number of new accounts closed _____

        Number of consulting days worked _____

    Special activities undertaken:

        1. _____

        2. _____

        3. _____

Objective for the next year

    Financial targets: Sales _____   Profit _____

    Special projects planned:

        1. _____

        2. _____

        3. _____

Long-range strategy

    _____

    _____

    _____

maximum and minimum tolerance lines on either side of the sales projection. Figure 2-5 shows this in graph form.

Should sales drop below the minimum line, major reductions in direct labor and overhead would be required. Sales above the maximum line might lead to cash shortages, out-of-stock items, late deliveries, and overtaxed personnel.

Long-Range Considerations

The starting point for the preparation of any long-range plan or strategy is, first, defining the kind of business you have now and, second, defining the kind of business you wish to have. Coming to grips with these definitions is often a painful process, mainly because all desired growth carries an element of risk. If you're the comfortable owner of a million dollar business, should you risk the money, effort, and insecurity of developing a new product? Perhaps you would really prefer to go along as you have in the past, secure in the knowledge that you're doing all right. This is

Figure 2-5.   Projected sales showing maximum and minimum tolerances.

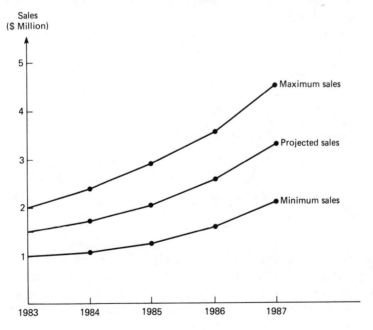

a decision that you have to make yourself, because it involves personal values and goals as well as company objectives.

Frequently, however, small businesses are forced into growth decisions by circumstances. Suppose, for instance, that you found your business increasingly dependent on one customer. In most cases, this would not be a comfortable or a healthy situation, and it would be wise for you to see how you could expand your business and thus lessen your dependence. Even so, growth is always difficult, not only for the owner but also for his employees.

> **Idea #14:   The pursuit of new products or the penetration of new markets means, to an employee, additional work and additional risk of failure without compensatory increase in pay or position.**

I'm sorry to say that there's much truth in this mordant observation, but of course it is certainly not the whole story. Growth can be an exciting and rewarding challenge to all your employees if you make an effort to communicate your own realistic hopes and plans for the future of the company. Communication always presents problems, but if you take the time and trouble to make sure that your employees know and understand your long-range goals, they may become caught up in the excitement and opportunity of growth and will support your goals wholeheartedly.

Growth-Minded Directors

> **Idea #15:   One of the most effective methods of stimulating growth is to select an active and imaginative board of directors.**

An enterprising board of directors forces the owner to be concerned with plans for growth. Without growth plans, the directors' meetings become nothing more than mundane social gatherings—a source of no help to the owner. It's good to have business

"I hate it when our board meeting erupts into a power struggle."

Cartoon by Howard Stringer, *Houston Business Journal*. Reproduced by permission of The Small Business Foundation of America, Inc., Editorial Cartoon Contest, 1979.

associates in similar but non-competitive firms as members of your board. As a rule they are more effective than family members or employees. Candidates can be neighbors with businesses of their own and friends met at business functions or seminars. Seminars, as a matter of fact, make an excellent hunting ground for board candidates. It's been my experience that seminar participants are the kind of people a growth-oriented company needs on its board. Interested in learning more about business and in improving themselves, they help provide the knowledge and ambition a growing company needs in its decision makers.

If you spot a likely candidate, don't be reticent about asking him or her to serve on your board. Many owners are, but in my experience such reticence always proves groundless. You will be amazed at how your offer pleases and how eager most people are to accept. At the same time, it's wise to be careful about including people in certain professions on your board. Accountants, bankers, consultants, and lawyers may have business dealings with your firm, its suppliers, or its customers, and conflicts of interest may arise. Board members should be paid an honorarium, of course— say, $100 to $200 per meeting—and it's sensible to take out liability insurance for each member.

Remember, you have chosen your board of directors for a specific purpose: to help stimulate the profitable growth of your company. Be sure all members clearly understand your annual sales plan and your long-range program and make every effort to be open to their suggestions and advice.

You've pinpointed your market targets. You've developed a realistic game plan. You've selected a board of directors eager and able to help. This is a solid foundation on which to grow. In the next chapter, we'll discuss another important consideration: "Achieving That Crucial Difference."

CHAPTER 3

Achieving That Crucial Difference

Why do your customers buy your product instead of your competitor's? What's the difference? Is it the quality of the product? Its price? Its packaging? The ability of your salespeople? Your company's reputation? Your advertising and promotion? Your speedy delivery? Your follow-up service?

All these factors are elements of *differentiation*, an important concept that you should clearly understand and incorporate into your marketing strategy.

> **Idea #16: Differentiating your product or service from the competition's should be incorporated into your strategy as a way of influencing the buyer.**

While on a recent trip to the drugstore for dental floss, I learned from the proprietor that Johnson & Johnson had the best selling dental floss in the store. This was surprising because it cost 70 cents more than the same quantity of another brand of dental floss. Why do people pay more money for the Johnson & Johnson product? Because they have confidence in the company, a confidence fostered by extensive advertising and effective distribution. There are hundreds of similar examples of companies

41

that gain a marketing advantage by differentiating their product from the competition's in the minds of the purchasers. Most of these are large national companies, which can afford the broad-based and persistent advertising and promotional campaigns that such differentiation requires, but the basic idea is really much the same for all companies, large or small. In fact, there are many ways of achieving differentiation that don't require large expenditures.

THE MARKET NICHE

Seeking out a niche and positioning yourself in it often proves to be an excellent way of avoiding direct competition with larger firms. This is an element of differentiation that often brings success.

A young, technically trained businessman named Michael Kinkead saw a marketing niche in the thrift industry (savings banks and savings and loan associations) back in 1974 when he observed that these institutions had no fully automated "back office" system for accounting, financial planning, and budget control. He also noted that the financial people (treasurer, comptrollers, and others) were forced to share the data processing department's main computer with the customer operations people, who had priority. Their only alternative was to use the services of an outside time-sharing company, which was costly and slow.

Here was a market niche nobody had tried to fill. It was too small for the computer companies to pursue directly, yet a need clearly existed. Why not, Kinkead asked, prepare a software program specifically for this market application, one that would be designed by the financial users, rather than by the data processing people? Kinkead's idea was to package this program with a mini-computer that could sit in the financial department and be operated by clerical personnel who had no knowledge of computer language or terminology. All they'd need would be some training on the operation of the keyboard.

Kinkead heard plenty of reasons why this idea wouldn't work from friends and advisers. Thrift firms, they said, wouldn't spend

$40,000 to $250,000 to automate their back office. But Kinkead went ahead with his plans.

In his first year, he sold two systems. Today he is one of Digital Equipment Corporation's largest distributors of minicomputers, with sales of $10 million and more than 100 employees. His company, the Saddlebrook Corporation of Cambridge, Massachusetts, has been growing at an average rate of 121 percent a year. Kinkead attributes his growth, in large measure, to his ability to focus on a market opportunity, a market niche, that nobody else had recognized. Once he identified the niche, he then provided a practical means of satisfying its needs.

Idea #17: **It's possible to succeed and grow without competing directly with larger firms by finding your special market niche.**

THE SELLING SPECTRUM

Don't be discouraged if you can't find a profitable market niche right away. Such safe pockets of business are not all that easily come by, and opportunities for differentiation exist in other areas. These areas, collectively known as the "selling spectrum," consist of seven sequential stages of sales development:

1. Product/service.
2. Packaging.
3. Pricing.
4. Advertising/promotion.
5. Buyer/buying process.
6. Delivery.
7. Follow-up service.

Study these seven steps. Each offers you an opportunity to differentiate your wares from those of your competition. Let's examine each step in detail as a possible element in your differentiation strategy.

Idea #18:   When a company effectively differentiates it-self from its competition at one or more of the stages of the selling spectrum, it creates sales and promotional opportunities.

Product/Service

The first point of differentiation is the product or service itself. A few products are one-of-a-kind, with no direct competition. This is an enviable position to be in, provided there are enough cus-tomers who buy the product. Most products face direct compe-tition, so it's wise to strive to differentiate your product in every way possible: quality, design, effectiveness.

Product differentiation is beautifully illustrated by the elec-tronic piano tuner. For years tuning forks have been used to tune pianos. When hit, the fork vibrates and creates a fixed tone used as a standard for adjusting the piano. Dr. Albert Sanderson, a professor of physics at Harvard University, asked the key question: Why should people depend on their fallible ears to tune pianos when electronics could do the job faster and more accurately? Dr. Sanderson invented an electronic tuner, which Gerald Volk, pres-ident of Tuners Supply Co., of Somerville, Massachusetts, helped develop into a marketable product. The tuner is $7^3/_4$ in. by 4 in. by 4 in., weighs 2 pounds, and looks much like a simple AM-FM radio. (See Figure 3-1.) When a note is played on the piano, lights tell the operator whether the instrument is in tune.

Sight-O-Tuners are now being successfully sold by mail order. They are much more expensive than simple tuning forks, but they do the job electronically with speed and accuracy. Probably no two devices that perform essentially the same task are more dis-similar than a tuning fork and a Sight-O-Tuner: a clear-cut example of differentiation in a centuries-old market!

But what about products that are not dramatically different from the competition? Differentiation can still be achieved. It's always possible, for instance, to pursue quality as a product's differentiating feature. Usually, that involves having the product

Figure 3-1. Electronic tool for tuning pianos. (Courtesy Tuners Supply Company.)

tested by standards-setting organizations and adhering to the quality requirements of a special market.

Al Horka, founder and president of the Plastic Extrusion and Engineering Company (PEXCO), took the differentiation-by-quality route in his marketing approach. Founded in 1960, Horka's company was one of several hundred firms making extruded plastic tubes. Naturally, price competition was severe—to consumers, one plastic tube is just like another.

Horka differentiated his tubing from others by promoting its medical and health care applications. (He was not unaware that this market discarded tubes after each use and replaced them with new tubes.) The medical market insists on top quality and stringent manufacturing requirements, and tube dimensions must meet tight tolerances. In addition, the manufacturer must assemble and maintain historical and production data, so that the Medical Devices Division of the Food and Drug Administration can identify, for recall, an entire production lot, should one tube be found defective or contaminated. The Agency is also seeking legislation requiring a "clean room" (controlled environment designed to minimize bacteria). The number of extruders willing and able to meet these requirements are few. By concentrating on this special market niche, PEXCO has been able to charge a much higher price for its tubes because they are successfully differentiated on the basis of quality in a highly competitive market.

Packaging

Packaging refers to the outer dress of the product, the exterior design, the container in which it comes, the way it is displayed. Physical package design is an art, particularly for a consumer product. Small companies should use a professional design consultant. This can be expensive, but you have an alternative:

> **Idea #19:   Check with your packaging supplier before investing money in design. Most medium to large packaging suppliers have their own designers who will give you free service in order to sell their products.**

Working with professional designers and copywriters demands your full attention. It's a mistake to give them the assignment and go away expecting them to create a package exactly right for your product. Work closely with them, describing in detail the selling benefits you want featured. Make suggestions about how the package should look. Give them samples of packages of similar products that appeal to you. In other words, be aware that even top professionals need all the input you can give them if the design is going to do an effective job of selling your product.

More often than not, a packaging concept will go through two or more stages in rough form before you get what you need. Don't hesitate to ask for revisions and even new concepts if you're not fully satisfied. Remember: That package will be helping to sell your product for a long time. Make it good!

> **Idea #20:   The copy and package design message should be clear, simple, and straightforward. Too much clutter obscures the message and thus the impact.**

Owners and managers often fall into the trap of insisting on much literal detail in copy and artwork. This is understandable because of their knowledge of all that's gone into the product's creation and production. For many products, however, such detail doesn't work in packaging. Always keep in mind that the package is a selling tool and should be designed accordingly.

Idea #21:   "Sell the sizzle and not the steak."

The emphasis of copy and artwork should be on illustrating, by word and picture, the user applications of your product—not the ingredients, brand name (unless it's nationally advertised), or instructions for use.

Above all, be sure your package design possesses a distinct differentiating quality. Research tells us that the average shopper spends 30 seconds or less looking over the variety of brands of a particular item before he or she makes a decision. Your package should be designed to give your product the edge in that crucial moment of decision. In a mass merchandising setting, the sales clerks offer the shopper little or no assistance. Therefore, a product's package must be an attention-getter.

Idea #22:   Strive for differentiation in your packaging, to set it off from better-known brands.

In-store promotions allow marketers to use the carton and shipper successfully as well as the display package. Keep in mind that if the carton is used for displaying the individual unit package, the units must be packed so that once a buyer has removed a few items, the unsupported remainder will not fall into disarray.

Idea #23:   If a carton is to be used for display, the exterior facing should be fully utilized to convey the sales message. Note: Make sure that the carton can be easily unpacked and set up by an untrained clerk.

A Packaging Success Story

Good packaging became one of the effective tools for helping the Gloucester Company's Phenoseal on the road to success. You may remember from Chapter 1 how the Gloucester Company switched from the marine market to the do-it-yourself homemaker. Its new distribution is through hardware and building supply chains. How could packaging help to positively differentiate Phenoseal from numerous other products, including those of Dow and General Electric?

Two techniques worked very well. The first was the preparation of a Day-Glo package that was open in the center, with pictures and copy highlighting the major end-use applications. This package accomplished three objectives, each of which helped differentiate Phenoseal from its competitors:

1. The Day-Glo stood out on a crowded shelf or display board, thus catching the shopper's eye.
2. The open package enabled the shopper to touch and squeeze the tube prior to purchase. The open package announced "this is what you get," and shoppers appreciated knowing.
3. The potential applications were illustrated on the package with the product name and company name.

The second technique of differentiation involved placing a blob of Phenoseal on a display stand header, so that the potential purchaser could feel the end product. Below this "blob" were small samples of metal, slate, and wood adhered to the header by Phenoseal to illustrate the various uses of the product. The shopper could see the product in its dry state and test its bonding properties.

Incidentally, Phenoseal got an added bonus from store managers who, when asked, would recommend it instead of better known competitors. Their reason: A lower percentage of Phenoseal than competitive products was returned by dissatisfied customers. Phenoseal's package and display lessened the customer's chances of making a mistake in selecting a product for household repairs.

Pricing

Pricing is a precisely stated and very important element of the selling spectrum, and one in which differentiation is often most crucial. In the customer's mind, the listed price indicates the comparative value of the product. But this sharp differentiation can be obscured by effective packaging and by unequal quantities between brands.

For example, in my previously mentioned trip to the drugstore, I looked at Procter & Gamble's 5 oz. spray can of unscented Super-Dry Sure, which retailed at $1.69. At that time, the druggist had received a spray can of the same diameter of *improved* unscented Super-Dry Sure to be retailed at the same price. In comparing these two identically priced products, I found that the old 5 oz. can was 5$^1/_2$ in. high, while the new can, which contained only 4 oz., was 7 in. tall!

Pricing of consumer products can be further obscured at the retail level with "price off specials," and at the wholesale level with similar specials, offers of dating or other payment terms, and extra merchandise in the form of "Get one free when you purchase 11" kinds of arrangements.

Pricing is just as important in the industrial market, particularly in securing penetration for new products.

Idea #24:   Most industrial products are sold on the basis of price, quality, and delivery. Since quality and delivery can't be fully judged until after the product has been bought, price becomes paramount in gaining acceptance for a new product.

This is why companies, large and small, will offer a potential customer a low introductory price. They want the prospect to try their new product. Once the product has been bought, the importance of price in relationship to other factors is diminished. That's when the price can be increased.

Idea #25: Before you try to improve your marketing position, make sure that you know your true costs for

each item sold and that your minimum price adequately covers these costs. Otherwise, you may expand yourself right into bankruptcy!

Advertising and Promotion

The key to differentiating through advertising and promotion is to play up the areas in which your product or service distinguish themselves in the marketplace. This may sound obvious, but it's important to mention because companies often do just the opposite, usually to their regret. Cleverness or creativity won't sell your product unless it's cogently related to the special features the product offers.

Sometimes a good advertising agency can be of great help in creating a new image for your company, provided that image is based on your products, services, or other elements in the selling spectrum. Always be sure that the agency you employ understands the specific media in which you need to have your company appear. Some agencies specialize in industrial products, others excel at penetrating consumer markets. It's wise to be sure that you're leaving the selection of the proper media for your product in the hands of experts in that field.

Buyer/Buying Process

A simple example of buyer differentiation is evident at an auto repair shop not far from my office. It is a small shop, capable of housing only two cars at a time, yet there is always a bustle of activity about the place. One can sense that the owner is earning a good income, even though his shop is small and unpretentious. Why?

The answer lies in the fact that many of the cars are antiques and classics. They are the owner's specialty, and he's recognized for his expertise. This expertise helps him develop additional business, because customers who bring their vintage cars to him also bring their late-model autos, and they also recommend him to their friends.

A more sophisticated example of differentiation in the buyer area comes from Al Hanlon, whose story was told briefly in Chapter 1. Hanlon's trade show exhibits are based on the theme "how to increase sales." So he makes his pitch not to a company's advertising manager, but to its sales manager, the person interested in increasing sales. The sales manager is not the traditional buyer of trade show exhibits, but Hanlon has had great success because he differentiates his services precisely by reason of their ability to make sales at trade shows. He offers customers sales training for booth personnel as well as a variety of exhibit designs and other services, all related to selling his clients' products.

Buyer differentiation allows many companies to penetrate special high-volume markets, two of which are the United States government and overseas customers. Both hold much promise for small businesses, but they are not pursued as vigorously by many as they might be, mainly because they are "different" and "require a lot of paperwork," according to the general opinion. But both markets are well worth pursuing, as we shall see in the detailed discussion and guide to their pursuit in Chapter 9.

Delivery

Prompt delivery is often underrated as a method of differentiation. It can be a particularly effective tool for industrial service companies, such as distributors. But, of course, prompt delivery ranks as an appealing plus for consumer products and services. For many companies it is about the only way to achieve effective differentiation.

Take, for instance, a television repair shop in my home town called General Electronic Services, managed by William Shriberg. One of the few means at Shriberg's disposal for distinguishing his service from that of his competitors is speed of delivery. So Shriberg offers both a one-day repair service on sets carried into his shop and prompt pickup and delivery for larger sets. Of course, simply offering rapid service isn't enough. Shriberg makes sure consumers know about it through ads in local newspapers, mailers, and word of mouth.

The New England foundry business illustrates the importance

of rapid delivery of items other than the finished product. A market study revealed that the largest single complaint among customers and prospects was the slow delivery, by a foundry, of quotations to customers. Most foundries considered the delay to be inevitable. After all, foundrymen are craftsmen, not pencil pushers! The preparation of a quotation is a time-consuming task, often involving sub-contractor quotations from pattern makers and other outside vendors.

Jim Hamblet, president of Foundry Technology Incorporated, made two changes in his firm's marketing procedure in order to distinguish his firm in this area. First, he assigned the responsibility for preparing quotes to a single individual. Second, he established the policy that quotations would be issued within ten working days of the receipt of the quote request. These two changes were instrumental in increasing sales by 25 percent during the six months following their introduction.

A final example is provided by Eagle Electric Supply Company, an electrical products wholesaler servicing the Greater Boston market. Eagle has been one of the fastest growing distributors in its market area. This growth has been accomplished in spite of its relatively limited parts inventory compared with its larger competitors. When Eagle gets an order for a part that is needed urgently by a prospect or a customer, but is neither in stock or is never stocked (a competitive line), Eagle locates the part at a competitor's facility, sends its delivery van to pick up the part and delivers it promptly to the buyer. While such a transaction may not be profitable in and of itself for Eagle, the positive impact on overall business has been tremendous. Buyers quickly learn that Eagle is eager to do business with them and can get any part when needed. A single source of supply!

Follow-up Service

The chance to differentiate does not cease when the sale has been completed and the goods or services have been delivered. Follow-up service still remains. Good follow-up service enhances a company's reputation and thereby helps to increase sales.

Large companies with local sales and service offices often have an advantage in this area of the selling spectrum. What can smaller companies do? Many are now offering toll-free "800" lines whereby customers experiencing difficulties with a product can call and get expert advice about repairs. Some companies subscribe to national repair services, but for many products the quality of such services leaves much to be desired. A spirit of helpfulness to customers and a willingness to act promptly in response to complaints counts a lot for small companies competing with the big national service staffs.

One of my clients often faces the problem of follow-up service. It is Tranti Systems, manufacturer of electronic cash registers. Tranti is too small (sales under $8 million) to offer locally based maintenance service centers on a nationwide basis, so it must convince prospects of its ability to respond rapidly to mechanical problems by other means. Tranti will dispatch a mechanic from the home office by plane or will instruct the user by telephone, and replacement parts are shipped air express.

Admittedly, though, Tranti encounters difficulties convincing prospective cash register buyers of its ability cope with competitors like National Cash Register, which does offer prompt service through local sales and service offices. So, at least until its service capabilities improve, Tranti should focus its energies and talents on other elements of the selling spectrum, and emphasize those that achieve the differentiation so necessary in today's marketing world.

CAN DISTRIBUTORS DIFFERENTIATE?

Distributors are tied to the product lines they represent, but they can achieve a measure of differentiation if they're willing to add to their product lines or replace one line with another. In this way, they can satisfy their customers and expand their business. Price, delivery, and service are the areas of the selling spectrum in which distributors generally strive for differentiation. But the distributor with marketing savvy keeps a constant watch on all seven areas of the selling spectrum for opportunities to get that extra thrust of differentiation that will help the company grow.

CAN SERVICE COMPANIES DIFFERENTIATE?

It's thought that a service company can best differentiate its "product" by specializing. Fast-growing consulting firms like Booze, Allen & Hamilton (which is, after Arthur D. Little, the second largest consulting firm in the United States) have maintained growth by offering increasingly specialized services.

The Venmark Corporation of Wellesley, Massachusetts, offers a "package" of publicity to the high-technology companies around Boston. Venmark was started a few years ago by Steven Stroum, who felt that the typical services of public relations and advertising firms were too vague and too expensive for many small business owners.

For a fixed fee of less than $500, Stroum sends a writer to a firm that has a new product to introduce. The writer gathers information and prepares a new product release. When the release is approved by the client, it is mailed to a pre-selected group of trade publications for inclusion in their "new products" section at no extra cost to the client.

This packaged service has proved very successful because of its low cost and its focused approach. Venmark has achieved product differentiation by offering a specific service that can readily be understood by potential buyers.

TAKE ANOTHER LOOK AT YOUR SELLING SPECTRUM

The selling spectrum provides seven essential areas in which your company can strive for differentiation and thereby find its strongest position on which to base future growth.

Idea #26: Selling should not be thought of as a single event (that is, the close of the sale), but as a continuing

process of linked elements, each building on the next in what is called the selling spectrum.

This concept is worth much study in your effort to achieve the crucial difference between your product or services and the competition. The next step is the sale itself. Successful selling combines art with sound management, as we shall see in the next chapter.

CHAPTER 4

The Art of Selling

In your company's approach to the complex art of selling, you as owner or manager play a crucial role. You organize the selling program, create the strategy, make the decisions. There's another possibility you may have overlooked: You are probably your firm's most effective salesperson.

Think about it. You have the status, experience, product knowledge, corporate understanding, and intuition about people. More important, you have the greatest motivation to raise profits and lower expenses. And you don't have to justify your actions to a boss, so you can devote as much time to a prospect as you think necessary.

With these advantages, you are wasting an invaluable asset if you do not give a good measure of your personal attention to selling. In any event, you certainly need to understand the techniques of selling, so that you can work successfully with salespeople and help them do a good job.

BREAKING DOWN THE PROCESS

Once you have located a prospect, there are just five stages in the selling process:

1. Identifying the decision maker.
2. Arranging the initial encounter.
3. Arousing interest.
4. Convincing the prospect.
5. Securing the close.

Identifying the Decision Maker

The first task in selling is to determine precisely who the buyer is. It's easy to waste a perfectly good sales presentation on the wrong person, but it happens all the time.

Idea #27:   Always make an extra effort to be sure you're calling on the person who will make the buying decision. Don't start too low in an organization, as many do. Be sure to call on the decision maker—not a subordinate.

This isn't snobbery, just common sense. It's difficult to move up once you've made the call, because the person you initially contact is often reluctant to have you go over his or her head. On the other hand, should you start too high, you will most likely be routed to the proper party without difficulty.

There's no formula for ascertaining on whom to call, but a good rule of thumb is: If in doubt, call at the higher level. When contacting a purchasing agent, try also to talk to the person who will be involved with your product when it's bought. That person usually plays a role in the purchasing decision, so you can't ignore him or her. But don't, in any case, ignore the purchasing agent, even if the user of the product has recommended yours.

One of my clients, the Engineering Sales Corporation (ENSACO) of Wellesley, Massachusetts, ran into a typical problem in this connection. Its technically trained sales personnel would "sell" to a prospect's engineering design department and the engineers would recommend purchase of ENSACO's products, but the purchasing agent would contact several other sources on an "ENSACO or equal" basis. Often one of the other firms would secure the order with a lower bid. Now ENSACO's salespeople sell to purchasing agents as well as to engineers. This doesn't assure them of the sale, but the purchasing agent will usually give ENSACO a "last look" at the competitor's price.

The intricacies of selling a product to more than one decision maker often require psychological perception as well as business acumen. Tranti Systems, the Massachusetts manufacturer of cash registers for fast food franchises mentioned in Chapter 3, found that the real buying influence was not the store manager, as had been assumed, but the franchisee's comptroller. Actually both had to be sold—but on quite different qualities of the product.

The store manager wanted a cash register that would do the bookkeeping, thus reduce after-hours computations. The comptroller didn't care about the manager's working hours, but looked for a better method of monitoring inventory, pinpointing losses, and determining which items were selling. Armed with the knowledge of these dual interests in the buying decision, Tranti's salespeople have modified their approaches. They make sure that the comptroller as well as the store manager hears their story. Group decision making is common practice these days, so the effective salesperson takes special care to touch base with everyone involved. In selling my own services, I've found that I rarely get a sale unless I personally meet and talk with all the partners of a business, preferably together, at some point in the selling process.

Arranging the Initial Encounter

Now's the time to gain the attention and respect of the buyer. Four suggestions:

First, call or write for an appointment. Even when a salesperson regularly calls on the same buyer, an advance contact accomplishes two things: It shows that you are professional enough to respect the buyer's time and it forces you to plan in advance what you will say.

Second, your meeting should have a specific purpose—perhaps it's to discuss the prospect's needs, display your samples, or give a demonstration. Even when contacting a buyer you see regularly, you should be able, with a little imagination, to have something new to discuss besides the latest ballgame scores. If your company doesn't have a "product of the month" program, create a product or concept idea of your own.

Third, make sure that you're dressed appropriately. Remember, 80 percent of what the prospect sees when looking at you is your clothes.

Fourth, open the conversation on a cheerful note, with a comment aimed at the buyer's personal interests, apart from the business at hand. Look for something interesting on the prospect's wall or desk as a possible subject. (And remember, you don't *have* to talk about the weather!) The idea is to put the prospect in a relaxed, receptive mood.

Arousing Interest

Obviously, you must get your prospect's attention if you are going to convince him or her of the value of your product or service. Concentrate on the *benefits* of what you're offering. Of course, on the initial call, you most likely won't know your prospect's needs, so be sure to ask. You might say, "In order for me to find out how I may best serve you, I'd like to ask a few questions . . . ."

The most sophisticated approach, one that an ENSACO salesperson might use on a technical prospect, is to offer to conduct a study (value analysis) of the company's product aimed at finding ways of reducing costs or improving performance. Offering a service of this kind at no extra charge is often an effective device for arousing interest, and it has an invaluable extra attached: It allows you to schedule a second visit to report your findings and drive home your sales message.

Convincing the Prospect

"Be brief, don't overtalk, be specific, and, above all, nail down each point." That's the prescription of Percy Whiting, the well-known author and managing director of the Dale Carnegie Sales Course. Your facts, presented in this manner, should demonstrate that your product or service will benefit the prospect and that he is justified in buying.

It's important not to spread your case too thin by amassing an overload of sales points. Your concentration on the key points is what convinces a prospect. All too often a conscientious salesperson will drag in dozens of selling features, producing a blur of talk which prevents the prospect from remembering any of the features. Highlight the strong points by discussing them as clearly and emphatically as you can.

Idea #28:   Concentrate your sales presentation on a few of the most salient points. Separate each point from the others, and drive it home with both a fact and a benefit.

Here, as an example, are three simple sales points and their benefits to the buyer. The salesperson could have brought in many others—product quality, product design, company status, and so on. Instead, he or she chose to concentrate on just three that were of particular interest to the prospect. Note that the selling feature or "fact" implies the "benefit." In the presentation, however, the salesperson clearly pointed out the relationship between fact and benefit. Don't depend on implication to convince your prospect. Spell it out!

Fact	*Benefit*
1. "Our firm has been in business since 1960."	"This means that you can be confident that we are a successful, dependable firm and that our warrantee has validity."
2. "We have done work for the Johnson Company."	"This means that we have specific experience on your exact applications."
3. "We are located within 30 miles of your plant."	"This means that our serviceman should be able to reach you within an hour in real emergency."

The next step in closing the credibility gap is to show the prospect what you're selling. In some cases, you may be limited to a visual display, as in a mail order catalog. For very large, hard-to-transport products, you may show the prospect a series of photographs or, better yet, a videotape of the product in action.

It's always best, of course, to bring the product with you whenever possible so the prospect can see, touch, and experiment with it. You may even leave it behind for a short time. People usually want to see an item before they will seriously consider purchasing it.

If you sell a tangible, operating product or a machine, a demonstration is probably your most effective tool, but there are problems with demonstrations that you should anticipate and try to avoid. The first is the salesperson's eternal problem: making sure the "right people"—the decision makers—are present. It's better to delay the demonstration until you have all the decision makers committed to attending than to put on several demonstrations for random gatherings. The decision makers should see your demonstration as a group so that your message will have a single impact.

The second problem arises when the product doesn't work as claimed. This surely makes for much embarrassment and more lost sales! But it happens. Make sure that the person giving the presentation has plenty of time to rehearse and that you've worked out all the bugs in the product.

A third difficulty is sometimes encountered when you take your prospect to a customer installation. This is often a good approach, but it has two or three possible disadvantages that should be anticipated. For one thing, the customer's product may not be functioning properly or it may be handling a job not related to your prospect's needs. The one big disadvantage of such visits, though, lies in the fact that you may lose control of the demonstration. The customer often takes over the conversation—and the demonstration—leaving you out in the cold, unable to make your sales pitch effectively. In spite of such problems, customer demonstrations remain a most effective sales tool and should be utilized whenever the opportunity arises, usually as reinforcement for the initial office demonstration.

Keep in mind that the most effective demonstrations are those tailored to the requirements of the prospect. In preparing your presentation, decide what specific benefits your product might offer the prospect. Then be sure to arrange for the prospect to become an active part of the demonstration. An effective technique is to set up an imaginary situation in which your product plays a decisive role. Here's a typical situation created for the demonstration of a copier:

"It's late in the day, a few minutes before five," you say, painting a word picture for your prospect. "Here comes Sally, the Sales Manager's secretary, with your weekly report. It has to be printed and mailed to the field by tomorrow!

"All you have to do is place the report, a page at a time, on your new copier, set the dial for the number of copies you need (let the prospect set the dial) and simply touch the button (let the prospect press the button) . . . ."

This approach may sound simple, but encouraging participation in a demonstration by a prospect has proven effective time and again.

Idea #29: Be sure to include some form of demonstration in your sales presentation. If at all possible, make it the kind of demonstration that invites participation on the part of the prospect.

For most products, especially for capital goods, the demonstration provides the impact to lift the buyer's level of interest to the point where you will make the sale. An astute salesperson tries to determine the prospect's level of interest at each stage, starting at the beginning of the relationship. Figure 4-1 shows how the level of interest varies through the stages of the sales procedure for an operational capital equipment item.

Idea #30: The ideal time to give a demonstration is when the prospect's real needs have been identified and

Figure 4-1. Buyer's level of interest throughout the sales procedure.

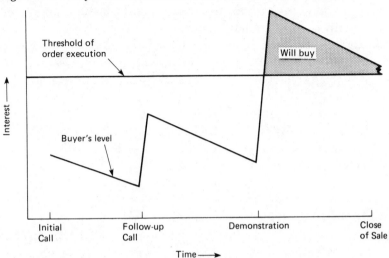

he or she has exhibited interest in your product. If the demonstration goes well, the prospect should be ready to make a commitment in your favor.

Securing the Close

When is your prospect ready to be asked for the order? Hundreds of articles have been written about closing techniques, and there are countless methods for determining the exact right moment, but in my experience these standardized formulas don't prove too helpful in the real world of buying and selling.

It's my conviction that once you have created a sufficient level of interest in the prospect, the close will fall into place naturally. If the required level of interest hasn't been attained, no amount of badgering or trial closes will get the prospect to place the order.

Idea #31: The close should be attempted as soon after the demonstration as possible. The longer you wait, the more the prospect's interest will decline.

When you think your prospect is ready to close, ask for the order. If that doesn't work, give the prospect some form of a proposal with a price quotation attached. A formal proposal is an effective selling tool; it highlights the product's benefits while lending authority and validity to your verbal claims. And, more important, it gives you a good reason to return and ask for the order a second time.

One last comment on closing. Don't take "no" for an answer right away. Always ask why your prospect has turned you down. Get the objections out on the table, answer them, and then ask once more for the order.

SELLING SERVICES

In most respects, selling a service presents the same problems and opportunities as selling a product. All the techniques discussed in this chapter apply to some extent. It's obvious, though, that many services cannot be demonstrated in the way that products can. Demonstrating a service usually entails showing samples of work done for another customer, complete with feedback about the benefits derived, references, and endorsements. Advertising agencies can show their portfolios and, if the account warrants it, may draw up an entire campaign for a prospective client. Most service salespeople can find similar ways of demonstrating their intangibles, but perhaps the most convincing display of what a service company can do lies in its past performance for other customers.

> **Idea #32:   Salesmanship is all important to the growth-minded service company. It's not what you sell but how you sell it that often determines your success. Stress benefits to prospect! Support with references! And be convincing!**

I know this to be true from personal experience. In Greater Boston, there were 79 marketing consulting organizations listed in the 1981 Yellow Pages. I'm pretty sure that my rate of growth and net income exceeds 95 percent of those listed, not so much because of the exceptional quality of my work (I hope that's one reason, but I know there are other very competent professionals in the field), but simply because I enjoy selling my services and, frankly, I'm good at it. One reason is that I listen carefully to the prospect's needs and then show how I can help.

How many people do you know who are highly competent at what they do but have been limited because of their inability to market themselves? In a service business, success almost always requires a heavy emphasis on personal selling.

WHO WILL DO THE SELLING?

If you as owner or manager aren't going to do all the selling, who is? You have many different types of sales representation available, each with its advantages and disadvantages and each available at various stages in the selling process. Fortunately, it's not an either/or situation. You can effectively employ a variety of avenues for your sales program, intermixing them to fit the needs of your particular markets. Let's look at the choices.

Direct Salespeople

All in all, employing your own salespeople (who are sometimes called factory salespeople) has much to recommend it. Unlike sales reps, they are on your payroll and work for your company alone; thus you have control over which prospects and customers they visit, what they say, and how frequently they make calls. You pay for these advantages, of course, as we shall see in detail in Chapter 6, but for many companies, direct salespeople are definitely the way to go.

Idea #33:   In general, direct salespeople are more effective at selling your product than sales representatives and should be employed wherever feasible.

Sales Representatives

But don't write off sales reps. They are an important part of the marketing scene. In 1980, some 30,000 rep agencies sold more than $200 billion worth of goods. A sales rep—sometimes called a manufacturers' agent—works for himself (or herself) or for a sales rep organization. You pay the rep a commission on the products sold, usually 3 to 10 percent and sometimes higher.

Reps are independent; they're tied to your company by a simple agreement that can usually be cancelled by either party with 30 to 90 days notice. Reps agree to provide coverage in a specific geographic territory for which you grant them exclusive rights for the duration of your agreement. They do not take title to the products they sell, nor do they do the billing. They have little to say about price or terms of sale and delivery, which are dictated by you, the supplier. They often try to provide emergency mechanical service, but usually maintain only a very minimal parts inventory.

Dealers

A dealer differs from a sales rep organization in that a dealer takes title to your merchandise, ships it, does the billing, and usually provides direct service. Dealers stock products, parts, and literature. Typically, a dealer will order enough product per shipment to qualify for the first price break off your list. A dealer makes 15 to 30 percent, as a rule, on sales of your products.

Stocking Representatives

A stocking rep maintains some product inventory, but usually does not take ownership of the product and does not bill customers. A stocking rep is something of a cross between a sales rep and a dealer. Stocking reps receive a commission on their sales slightly larger than they might expect if they did not maintain inventory.

Distributors

The distributor takes title to your product (paying 40 to 50 percent less than your suggested price list) and resells it to the purchaser, end user, or original equipment manufacturer (OEM). The distributor handles industrial accounts, providing risk-free, local representation in a given geographic area. You simply ship your product to the distributor with an invoice, and back comes the check. No selling problems! But there's a hitch, which we'll discuss later in this chapter.

Wholesalers

Wholesalers have much in common with distributors, except that a wholesaler sells to a dealer, who then sells the product to the consumer market. Distributors sell directly to the OEM manufacturer in the industrial market; wholesalers sell indirectly in the consumer market. The words "distributor" and "wholesaler" are used interchangeably in many industries.

Cooperative Buying Organizations

This type of organization is a wholesale establishment owned and operated by retailers. The hardware industry furnishes a good example. Cooperative buying groups provide independent hardware retailers with the opportunity to compete with chain stores in buying power by pooling their numbers to obtain better prices. Best known is True Value® brand name of Cotter & Company of Chicago, which is owned by more than 6,000 franchised dealers.

What Kind of Representation for You?

Proper representation generally results from the interplay of four factors:

1. *Size of your firm.* Smaller firms, particularly those with annual sales under $5 million, tend to rely on reps more than larger firms.

2. *Your product line.* Capital equipment items and complex technical services are usually sold directly to end users, whereas components for the OEM market and commodities are more likely to be sold through reps.

3. *Trade practices.* Most industries have evolved character-

istic practices in regard to representation, and you are probably familiar with those in your industry. If you have an unorthodox idea for representation, there's no reason why you shouldn't give it a try. It may seem risky, but breaking with tradition often leads to success.

4. *Sales per customer.* The dollar amount of sales per customer should influence your decision on whether to employ a direct salesperson or a rep. Where a single average order is several hundred dollars or more, it makes sense to use a direct salesperson. Lower amounts per order call for a rep as the more cost-efficient choice for a single manufacturer.

Intermixing types of sales representation is common practice. It's always wise to keep an eye out for different kinds of representation and channels of distribution. Manufacturers often distribute one product through one channel and a second product through another. Or, more commonly, a manufacturer may use one form of selling in one geographic area and another form elsewhere.

How complex such arrangements can be is seen in Figure 4-2, which graphically represents the sales and distribution strategy of a well-known hand-tool manufacturer who sells to the national mass merchandising market.

PLANNING A DISTRIBUTION STRATEGY

It's easy to see that the variations involving sales representation are infinite. In planning a strategy to meet the needs of your particular markets, you should consider all possibilities, but you can't go far wrong by concentrating on the three major types available—direct sales, sales reps, and distributors (or in the case of consumer products, wholesalers).

Direct Salespeople or Reps?

If you can afford to hire direct salespeople, the advantages in most instances outweigh the disadvantages. Your control over their sales efforts generally makes for greater efficiency. The disadvantages are simply economic, not only in terms of the cost of

Figure 4-2.   A complex distribution process.

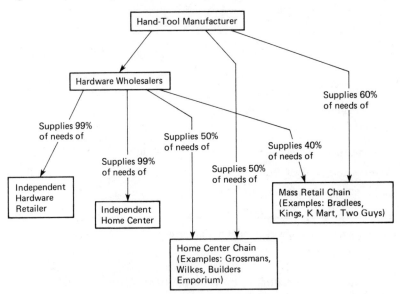

salary and benefits but also in terms of training and field expenses. Usually, as we said earlier, small companies with low-volume sales per customer favor sales reps who are paid solely on commission.

Beyond a certain point, however, using sales reps instead of direct salespeople can be a false economy. Table 1 is prepared from sales data from seven former SALESMARK clients. These firms, all custom manufacturers, had annual sales ranging from $886,000 to $6,800,000.

The key figures on this chart are the total cost per direct salesperson as a percentage of manufacturer's sales (3 percent) and the total rep commission as a percentage of manufacturer's sales (7.9 percent). The difference in cost to the manufacturer weighs heavily in favor of the direct salesperson when the volume of sales is high.

Idea #34:   In your company's home territory, use direct salespeople, not reps.

Table 1.   Sales data of seven New England manufacturers.

Category	Average	Range
Sales per direct salesperson	$926,000	$881,000–$971,000
Total cost per direct salesperson*	28,000	22,900–32,000
Total cost per direct salesperson as percent of net manufacturer's sales*	3%	1.4%–3.9%
Net sales per rep agency	$94,000	$59,000–$151,000
Commission paid to each rep agency	7,500	4,600–10,400
Total rep commission as percent of manufacturer's sales	7.9%	

*Includes travel and entertainment but *not* overhead or fringe benefit costs.

Your home territory should be your most productive territory; if you can't afford a direct salesperson there, then you, the owner or manager, should do the selling yourself. The potential of your home territory (which may comprise one city or several states) should be $1 million or more to warrant hiring a full-time salesperson.

The great advantage of sales reps, of course, is that you pay only for what you get. Many small companies rely on reps exclusively and with apparent success. However, in my 12 years of consulting I have met only one corporate owner who said he was completely pleased with his rep force. This isn't really surprising—a rep can't be tightly controlled. You're not the boss as far as a rep is concerned. But before rejecting reps out of hand, consider these pluses:

- Reps present no expense when orders drop off due to uncontrollable economic or business turns or seasonal sales fluctuations.
- Reps work as hard as—and often harder than—direct salespeople, because their commissions depend on it.
- Reps often have close ties to the buyer.

William T. Diamond, in *Distribution Channels for Industrial Goods* (Columbus, OH: Ohio State University Press, 1963, pp. 28–36), lists seven conditions under which a sales rep should be used:

1. The manufacturer has limited financial strength and cannot organize and maintain his or her own sales force.
2. A single product or narrow product line of low unit value is produced by the manufacturer.
3. The product is subject to wide cyclical fluctuations in demand (for example, Christmas tree ornaments).
4. The market is at a great distance from the manufacturer, making direct sales cultivation too expensive.
5. Prospects and customers are widely scattered, and travel costs for a manufacturer's sales force are therefore excessively high.
6. A new product is being marketed or a new market is being entered, and the agent's established contacts and prestige can be immediately and advantageously used.
7. Expansion of territorial coverage is desired, but potential is too low to justify adding to the manufacturer's direct sales force.

Idea #35: Successful sales reps work for their customers and only secondly for the manufacturers whose lines they carry. Try to utilize their rapport with customers to benefit your sales.

Table 2 sums up the differences between a direct sales force and manufacturers' agents or sales reps. It can be used as a guide to decision making in an important aspect of your sales program.

What About Distributors?

Distributors or wholesalers allow you to avoid most sales problems—they do all the work! There's a hitch, of course: You lose much control over the selling process. Your product is one

Table 2.   Comparison of direct salespeople and manufacturers' agents.

Item	Direct Salespeople	Manufacturers' Agents
Cost (compensation)	Direct salary expense. Fringe benefits include social security, health insurance, pension, vacation, and sick leave. Overhead includes office space, travel expense, training, sales meetings, and so on.	Paid on commission, usually computed as a flat percentage of sales. Rate depends on nature of product, agency practices, and any incentive scheme written into the contract.
Control	You have full control of a direct sales force and its selling approach.	You have much less control, even if your contract with agency specifies certain features of the sales program.
Training	New salespeople must be trained, often at great expense. Several years' work may be necessary to gain sufficient experience, and once trained, a salesperson can take those skills to another company.	Agents must know their territory and industry in order to make a living. May require training to handle your product, especially if it is highly technical.
Selling time	Selling time is devoted exclusively to your products.	Agents sell products for many companies. But several agents, each working only part time on your product, may generate more sales time than a full-time, direct salesperson.
Knowledge of inventory	Direct salespeople can take months or years to learn about a new territory and build contacts. Valuable experience and contacts are lost if salesperson leaves your company.	Experienced agents offer instant experience and contacts in a territory. No investment in building experience is required of your company.

Table 2. (*Continued*)

Item	Direct Salespeople	Manufacturers' Agents
Your product	Some products require special touches that a direct sales force can guarantee.	Because of your lack of control, it is much more difficult to make sure special touches are provided.
Return on investment	As a salesperson becomes more experienced, higher salaries are necessary. If the person's territory must be enlarged to pay the higher salary, and the call frequency and penetration are reduced as a result, your return will decrease.	You pay only on the basis of results. Your return is "guaranteed" in that you have to pay a commission only when the agent has made a sale.

(Source: "Should You Sell Through Manufacturers' Agents?" *Business Monthly*, June 1978. Reprinted with permission. © United Media International, Inc. All rights reserved.)

of hundreds the distributor may carry, and generally the distributor's salespeople have little knowledge of your product's special characteristics or selling features. So don't expect sales miracles from your distributors, particularly when introducing a new product.

Typically, a distributor's salespeople simply ask customers "What do you need today?" and don't make an effort to sell your product. Their best selling tool is their "line card," which lists all the products of all the manufacturers represented by the distributor.

On the other hand, distributors can do things for your sales that no other kind of sales representation can. If you manufacture a component for a system, for instance, your distributor can couple that component with others to make a complete package for customers. Your distributors can also supply a local inventory for your parts and provide service to customers.

Here are the conditions under which a distributor should be used, as listed by William T. Diamond in *Distribution Channels for Industrial Goods*:

1. The number of potential users of a given product is large and scattered geographically.
2. The unit value of the sale is low.
3. Prompt delivery and economics of shipment are important to customer. There is more than one delivery point per customer (for example, chain store warehouses).
4. Little or no technical sales service is required but prompt repair service may be important.
5. The manufacturer is small in size or can otherwise benefit from the "collection muscle" wielded by the distributor on accounts receivable.
6. The product is a commodity purchased on a regular basis for OEM use (for example, a subassembly part for a machine).
7. Industry customs dictate the use of distributors.

Idea #36: In diverse, geographically large markets where there is a minimal price competition, manufacturers should consider having two or more distributors carrying the same line.

Idea #37: Identify your prospective distributors on the basis of three traits: Do they have an aggressive sales program? Do they carry recognized product lines? Do they maintain tight overall controls, especially in the financial and inventory areas?

In planning your sales representation strategy, keep in mind the strengths and the weaknesses of the various methods available. Selling is an art that requires psychological insight, intuition, and hard-headed planning. It isn't necessary to be a born salesperson, or to have one on your staff, to manage a successful sales program. It is necessary, however, to approach the selling process with common sense, utilizing the techniques and resources readily available to everyone willing to make the effort.

CHAPTER 5

Managing Sales Territories

Managing territories involves three of your most valuable assets: time, money, and opportunity. If your salespeople have to travel great distances between calls, they are probably not covering their regular customers adequately, are incurring high travel expenses, and are too busy getting from place to place to develop new leads. Sound management of territories helps maximize sales and profits by giving you greater control so that you can organize your firm's selling efforts most efficiently. Determining which accounts get called on and when and how often the calls are made is a key decision in any company. That decision rests to a large extent on the way you manage and structure your sales territories.

Idea #38: Sales territories should be established primarily on the basis of market potential and secondarily on the basis of existing sales.

A FORMULA FOR ESTABLISHING SALES TERRITORIES

Here is a practical formula, adaptable to any kind of business, that appeared in *Sales & Marketing Management:* *

* Thayer C. Taylor, "The 1979 Survey of Industrial Purchasing Power," *Sales & Marketing Management,* April 23, 1979, pp. 3–10. ©1979. Reprinted by permission.

Step 1: Compile a list of your key accounts (the 20 percent that contribute 80 percent of your sales) and their sales for the last calendar year.

Step 2: Use Dun & Bradstreet's *Million Dollar Directory* (or an equivalent source) to determine the primary four-digit SIC code numbers for *each* of these accounts.

Step 3: Identify the major and most common SIC categories— the 20 percent that cover 80 percent of your key accounts.

Step 4: Develop a ratio for the two (or more) largest SIC code categories. This ratio represents the portion of your type of product used per $1,000 output of that SIC-coded industry.

For example, *S&MM* cites the case of an electronic components manufacturer. For every $1,000 of output in the motor vehicles industry, SIC 3711 requires $4.23 of the manufacturer's product; for every $1,000 of output in the aircraft industry, SIC 3721 requires $21.16 of the product.)

Step 5: Using *S&MM*'s industry survey section, you can determine the total shipments for that industry in the most recent calendar year. (In the above example, the motor vehicle industry shipped $85,238 million of product in 1978 and the aircraft industry shipped $18,310 million).

Step 6: Multiply these totals by your ratios for each industry and divide your own sales by these approximate industry totals to get your market share. (Our electronic components manufacturer found that there was a potential of $361 million in his product category among automobile manufacturers and $387 million among aircraft manufacturers. He then divided his own sales by these approximate industry totals to determine his market share nationwide.)

Step 7: After repeating this process for all key customer industries, rank them according to their relative market shares. This will indicate the markets that you have successfully penetrated and those that you haven't and will show you where considerable market potential exists.

Step 8: Using the county breakout from *S&MM*'s "Survey of Industrial Purchasing Power," *County Business Patterns* of the U.S. Bureau of Census, or Economic Information Systems computer data base (all available at most business libraries), determine the number of plants, volume of shipments, number of customers, and relevant sales in each county for each SIC number. Compare those figures with your existing coverage and sales figures. (The electronic components manufacturer found that salespeople were calling on all prospective accounts in Arizona, Pennsylvania and Vermont; were not doing as well in California and Connecticut; and were failing completely in Florida.)

Step 9: On the basis of either *potential* dollar sales or number of accounts (but preferably not on the basis of existing sales), divide up the territories. Remember to subtract house accounts first and to be certain that the remaining sales potential exceeds $1 million for each salesperson assigned therein.

Companies with under $10 million in sales, fewer than 10 salespeople, and regional coverage may wish to employ only steps 1, 2, 3, 8, and 9. Steps 4 through 7 require research that might be more complex than most smaller companies are willing to undertake.

For smaller companies that use sales reps, establishing territories can be quite simple. The rep has already established the territory, and the company benefits from his or her contacts.

Idea #39:   Assign a rep a geographic territory consistent with the territory he or she now covers for other manufacturers.

If you assign a rep a larger territory than he or she normally covers, you probably won't get effective representation outside the normal calling area. The rep will receive extra commissions for existing customers, but you won't benefit from the arrangement.

Assigning a rep a smaller-than-normal territory doesn't make much sense either. Some manufacturers will divide up a normal-size territory into two parts, placing one rep in each. They do this for one of two reasons: Either they have found two good reps and can't decide between them, or they want twice the coverage "horsepower" for the total area. Dividing a territory in this way is almost never a good idea. For one thing, the reps don't like it, so they may not push your product even in the territory to which they've been assigned. Remember, reps make their living handling several product lines. They can and do neglect manufacturers they aren't interested in or have a grudge against.

Another danger of the divided-territory approach is that the rep may be tempted to take on a competitive product in the other half of the territory. Or, when the opportunity arises, the rep may drop your line and work for a competitor who offers the entire territory.

When companies employ both reps and direct salespeople, they sometimes try to divide up product lines, having reps and direct salespeople coexisting in the same territory. This doesn't work either. Usually the rep feels like a second-class citizen, because the more profitable products or the exciting new ones are usually given to the direct salesperson and the rep is left with the balance. More important, the duality of company representation confuses customers. They often don't know whether to call the company's direct salesperson or the rep.

PLANNING TERRITORIES FOR DIRECT SALESPEOPLE

When you employ your own sales staff, managing territories entails significant decisions. The most important is deciding whether to assign accounts and prospects on the basis of geographic boundaries or on the basis of industry groups (such as hospitals, government agencies, insurance companies) and types of manufacturing firms. There are advantages and disadvantages to each approach, and one does not exclude the other. Many companies manage territories of both kinds, depending on their particular circumstances. Let's look at the basic considerations:

Geographic Approach

Territories are carved out geographically under the following circumstances:

- Customers and prospects are spread out over a large area.
- You want to minimize travel expenses. (However, this re-

sults in salespeople being less versed in operating proce-
dures of major industry segments.)
- Product applications are generally similar in nature.
- The purchasing agent is the dominant buying influence.
- The limited size of the market justifies only a few salespeople.

For a statistically minded manufacturer or distributor, county
or state lines provide the best boundaries for sales territories because SIC figures are available to determine market potential and
penetration. Market support personnel, on the other hand, favor
using U.S. Post Office zip code territories, for two reasons: They
cover a smaller geographic area than counties, and it is easier to
determine, when a prospect calls in, who the responsible salesperson is (the market support person simply asks the account for
the zip code). Salespeople themselves usually favor geographic
boundaries that are visually definitive demarcation lines—state
boundary lines, major highways, and rivers, for example. These
enable them to tell quickly from out in the field whether a prospect
is or is not in their territory.

In many companies all three ways of defining territories are
used concurrently. Outlying or sparsely populated territories are
distinguished by state or county boundaries. Suburban territories
are circumscribed by county lines and major reference points.
Large urban areas are divided by zip codes within counties.

**Idea #40:   If you're considering dividing a territory into
several smaller ones, do it now. Then, assign two or more
territories to a salesperson temporarily.**

This prevents a major morale problem later when a salesperson is told that his or her territory will be decreased in size.

**Idea #41:   If you find it advisable to alter or reduce a
salesperson's existing territory, give that person a 90-day
commissionable hold on, say, the 8 to 12 largest accounts
in the territory to be given up. You might want to have**

the salesperson keep one, two, or three of these accounts
permanently.

INDUSTRY APPROACH

Here are the features of a territory formed on the basis of
accounts within a particular market segment. Although it's a
widely used approach, the geographic method is more common.

- Customers are densely clustered in a major metropolitan
  area.
- A few key industry groups that account for a significant
  portion of sales have been identified.
- Salespeople can develop expertise in one or more given
  industrial areas or specialties.
- Each industry has its own unique operating system.
- The dominant buying influence is not the purchasing agent.
- The company has more than six salespeople.

One of the major advantages of the industry approach is that
your salespeople can be trained in the nuances of a particular
industry or group of industries. By focusing on particular industries, your firm can develop a reputation for excellence in those
market segments.

A major disadvantage of the industry approach is that such
territories usually cover a wider physical area than geographic
territories, so there's more driving time, less time for calls, and
greater expense all around. There's always the possibility, too,
that a salesperson may become such an expert in a given industry
that he or she will start an independent business serving the field.

It's good practice to give your most promising industry group
to a skilled, senior salesperson. That market is sure to represent
a prime target for your competitors, so you need to give it your
best shot. In addition, the senior salesperson is better equipped
to handle the large, complex orders of such accounts.

In deciding whether to go with the industry approach, consider the number of calls a salesperson can make in a day. In my

experience, an average of four to eight calls is advisable, with the actual number depending on the type of product or service sold. Strike a balance between the break-even cost of your sales effort in a particular market segment (a figure applicable to many industries would be to budget 10 percent of total sales revenues to cover salary, fringe benefits, commission, and expenses) and the number of active and potential accounts. You might find, for example, that a compact, geographically divided territory contains over 300 current accounts generating more than $1,200,000 in sales and that 40 of these accounts, representing more than $200,000 in revenues, were from a common type of business. That particular segment could form the basis of an industry territory ($200,000 × 10% = $20,000, a reasonable startup investment to cover the costs of a new industry salesperson).

Successful sales organizations devote much time and attention to managing territories, because it can be a decisive area. Surprisingly, however, many companies neglect it. A survey by the Sales Executive Club of New York showed that half the respondents never conducted an organized survey of their salespeople's use of time, a quarter had no system for classifying accounts by their potential, and almost three quarters had never attempted to set profit objectives for their accounts. By managing territories aggressively, you can get the jump on your competition.

Whether you take the geographic approach, the industry approach, or a combination of both, you should know as precisely as possible how much time and money go into your efforts to service your regular customers and to develop new ones. Keep in mind, too, that decisions about territories are best made before hiring a salesperson or engaging a rep. The territory helps define the job and the kind of person you need to do it well. And that brings us to the next topic: how to find, hire, and pay salespeople.

CHAPTER 6

Finding, Hiring, and Paying Salespeople

In sales, to paraphrase Vince Lombardi, good people aren't everything—they're the only thing. The quality of your salespeople directly affects the growth of your firm, because every prospect or customer regards a salesperson as an extension of your company and how it does business. A buyer may develop negative impressions of your firm if there is a high turnover of sales personnel, if sales presentations are weak, if a salesperson doesn't follow through, or if a salesperson displays inadequate product knowledge or even bad manners.

Admittedly, even the most diligently conducted hiring process cannot assure you of finding a good salesperson. But if you are careful you should improve your ratio of success.

All right. How should a salesperson be hired?

FINDING THE RIGHT PEOPLE

Preparing a Good Job Description

Even if no one else in your firm has a written job description, you should prepare one for each salesperson. Job duties may span several areas and may be likely to change, so a salesperson usually wears many hats—he or she may take inventory, coordinate trade show participation, and prepare literature. A job description is valuable because:

1. It forces the owner and sales manager to crystallize their thoughts about what the salesperson is expected to accomplish.
2. It gives the salesperson a clear idea of what duties management expects him or her to perform.
3. It provides both management and the salesperson with an important tool to be used in the annual performance review in determining how much, if at all, to increase the base salary.

A job description can be prepared in several different ways, but I prefer first to provide a general description of the function and then to list the duties to be performed. (Figure 6-1 provides an example of a job description for a distributor's salesperson.) I then describe the necessary background qualifications. On the basis of the job description shown in Figure 6-1, the XYZ Company might require the following qualifications:

1. *Education:* High school diploma, plus associate degree in any field of engineering.
2. *Experience:* Minimum two years of successful industrial sales experience in home office or field.
3. *Current earnings:* Under $20,000 per year.

Idea #42: Tell your employees precisely what you expect from them. Most companies don't, and the results are confusion and lowered morale.

Conducting the Search

Once the job description has been prepared, the type of applicant desired has been identified, and the compensation program has been established, it is time for the search to begin.

Figure 6-1.   Sample job description.

JOB TITLE: Salesperson.

FUNCTION: Represent company in the assigned territory (Northern
Illinois and Wisconsin, as defined on the attached map) by calling on
prospects and customers to sell pneumatic systems and components.
Reports to sales manager.

SPECIFIC DUTIES:

1. Meet or exceed mutually agreed-upon gross margin sales quota.

2. Continually seek out prospects for new accounts using manufacturer's
    (supplier's) leads, our leads, and referrals. Develop own leads
    by using reference materials and by "smoke stacking" (that is,
    visually spotting prospective companies).

3. Visit at least six new prospects each week. Call on both design
    engineer and purchasing agent. Acquaint them with our various
    product lines, find out their needs, and, if they are potential
    prospects, start asking for an order. An average of one new
    account should be closed each week.

4. Call on existing customers on a regular basis--once every two weeks
    for an "A" account, once a month for a "B" account, and when
    requested for a "C" account. Seek to establish new applications
    for our products and provide technical and service support as
    needed.

5. Make six to eight calls on prospects and/or customers each working
    day.

6. Regularly attend weekly sales meeting. Bring Weekly Call Plan for
    upcoming week and completed Call Report and Expense Summary from
    preceding week.

7. Report on competitive activities.

8. Participate in other projects as assigned by sales manager.

Idea #43:   An employer should try to obtain as many applicants as possible for each open job.

You should receive a minimum of 30 applications for any line sales function in home office or field and between 50 and 100 applications for any sales management or marketing supervisory function. There are two reasons why you should strive to review so many applications: (1) the more applications you evaluate, the greater the likelihood that you'll find and hire a superior individual. (2) The more applications you evaluate, the more likely that you will determine precisely what type of person is needed to fill the particular job.

It may seem to be a burden to screen and interview such a large number of applicants, but remember, people are your most important commodity. To find applicants, use as many sources as you can: newspapers, employment agencies, employee referrals, and customer referrals. Here are some practical suggestions for each source.

Newspaper Employment Ads

Your best bet is a Sunday and weekday combination run for just one week in your city's major employment newspaper. Trade publications are inexpensive places to advertise, but usually produce few applicants. Invest a few extra dollars to purchase a sizable ad measuring *at least* $2^3/_4$ in by 4 in. to attract a staff person; $2^3/_4$ in. by 5 in. for a salesperson, and 4 in. by 4 in. for a manager. Ask your agency, or whoever designs and inserts the ad, to include your firm's logo, to enclose the ad in a distinctive or heavy border, and to request placement in the upper right-hand portion of the Sunday employment page.

Idea #44:   Include in the copy of every ad the compensation rate or range for the job (a "must" to attract the right applicants). Include a phone number where you can be reached on Sunday afternoon, if the ad runs on Sunday. This attracts applicants who are not yet in the job market and may not have résumés prepared. Give the job the most prestigious title within reason.

Employment Agencies and Search Firms

An employment agency, often called a "personnel agency," interviews candidates who are looking for jobs, classifies them according to their abilities, and sends along the best prospects when you call about an opening. Its fee typically ranges from 10 percent to 35 percent of the starting salary. An executive search firm or executive recruiter (commonly known as a "headhunter") is an organization hired by an employer to find a well-qualified person for a specific position.

The most significant difference between the two is that a headhunter gets a retainer whether or not the search is successful. A personnel agency gets paid (sometimes by the job seeker, but increasingly often these days by the employer) only when the job is filled. Search firms are normally used to secure executive positions paying $30,000 a year and up. However, many employment agencies do handle executive positions. It's a good idea to keep in mind that employment agencies tend to send you as many candidates as they can, including those with less-than-ideal qualifications. They are not as discriminating as search firms, and thus you may find yourself spending more time than you care to interviewing unlikely applicants.

Here are some guidelines for dealing with employment agencies:

- Contact an agency only *after* you have received responses from your newspaper ad. That way you'll avoid paying a finder's fee for someone who would have contacted you anyway.
- Use two to three agencies. Make certain, however, to date-stamp all resumes forwarded by agencies. If the same applicant is referred by more than one agency and you are interested in the person, notify the second agency at once in writing that the person was already referred to you. Otherwise, you may receive two agency invoices at the time of hiring.
- Deal with just one person in an agency, preferably the owner.
- Visit each agency (or have a representative visit you). Pro-

vide the agency representative with a detailed job description, and discuss your preferences about personal characteristics of the applicants.

- If the agency turns out to be a "body shop" that sends you résumés of obviously unqualified applicants, stop using that agency. If not enough applicants are forthcoming or if the flow becomes a trickle, call regularly to remind the agency that the job is still open. Finally, when you fill the job, be sure to tell the agency.

- Find out whether your fee will be partially or completely refunded if an agency-referred applicant is fired within the first 90 days.

- Finally, remember that an agency is biased in favor of placing applicants; that's the way it makes a profit. Thus it may not have your interests of a long-term employer-employee relationship at heart.

Referrals

Recommendations from employees, friends, and business associates can prove to be an excellent source of one or two very capable candidates, particularly for lower-level sales administration positions. The higher-level positions usually require particular skills not usually found in referral candidates. At the lower level, experience and skill are not as important, and this level is where a referral can be of greatest benefit. So encourage referrals, but *don't* pay employees cash for referrals. A personal thank-you note should suffice. In this connection, I don't think it's a good idea to permit relatives to be brought onto your payroll. If an employee's relative is hired, then later fired, at least one person still on your payroll will be upset.

Screening Applicants

The next step is screening. All applications should be submitted in writing, and you should obtain an outline of the applicant's schooling and job history. It is not important whether the résumé itself is typed or handwritten, but it is important that every applicant submit a written document, including people who have called you on the telephone in response to a newspaper ad.

> **Idea #45:   Primarily on the basis of their résumés, screen all applicants, even those you have interviewed before and those who were referred to you. Do not hire a sales representative, sales manager, or marketing manager who has not been through a full screening process.**

Narrow down the number of applicants to between *eight* and *twelve* qualified, particularly promising candidates. The winnowing process can be accomplished by retaining only those applicants who meet the minimum required job specifications, have demonstrated an upward progression from one job to the next, and show employment solidity with an average of three or more years on each of the last three jobs (if the applicant has held that many).

Conducting Interviews

Preliminary Interviews

The eight to twelve chosen applicants should be contacted and invited in for a short get-acquainted session. Allow about 20 minutes to ask the candidate questions and ten minutes to explain the job. You will probably make your decision about the chemistry between the two of you within the first five minutes. His or her appearance, manner of speech, and personality will all be part of this initial image.

Final Interviews

Invite between four and six applicants back for a final in-depth interview conducted by you and at least one other member of your staff. If you have fewer than four people, continue the search until you find more.

In this detailed interview, which will probably last about an hour and a half, set aside the written application and ask the candidate to talk in some detail about every full-time job he or she has held and about major personal developments. Look for "success indicators" such as elected positions at school or awards, prizes, and commendations in sales work. Watch out for inconsistencies. Make certain that the applicant specifies dates of employment (including months), so as not to leave out short-tenure jobs.

Ask the applicant open-ended questions such as:

"What are your business and personal goals for the next 10 years?"

"What do you judge to be the most significant occurrence of your business career? Why?"

"What are your outside interests? Tell me about your hobbies. Do you participate in community activities?"

"What do friends and business associates consider to be your major strengths and weaknesses?"

Idea #46:   The response to the question about strengths and weaknesses may provide you with more insight into the applicant's personality than any other question in the interviewing process.

When you've gotten to know the applicant reasonably well, it's time to talk about the company and the job. Tell him or her your firm's strengths and weaknesses, describe the job's duties in detail and mention opportunities for advancement. Be honest. Remember that the person you hire will invest a portion of his or her life with your firm. Don't describe the position in detail until you have asked all of your interview questions. That will minimize the applicant's ability to slant responses to suit the situation.

Don't forget that at least one of your other employees (preferably two) should also interview the job candidate. Their participation will provide you with different points of view, will give them a stake in the new employee's success by involving them in the selection process, and will give the applicant a better picture of your firm. On the basis of the in-depth interviews, you should be able to select two to four candidates who could perform the job and who would be welcome additions to the firm.

Checking References

The next step is to check the references of the final candidates. Telephone at least two previous employers (*not* friends or business associates, but former *supervisors*) for each applicant. Ask about strengths and weaknesses. A key question to pose is "Would you rehire this former employee?"

In probing the applicant's previous job performance and ascertaining why he or she left, you should note not only what the former employer says and how he says it, but also what he does *not* say. The level of enthusiasm or bitterness is important.

Idea #47: Confidential telephone references from the applicant's former supervisors are one of the most important elements of the hiring process and may be the best indication of the applicant's potential success with your firm.

HIRING A NEW SALESPERSON

On the basis of the interviews and the reference checks, two top candidates should be selected and ranked as your first or second choices. All other candidates should be notified promptly, by mail or by telephone, that they are no longer being considered for the position. A sample rejection letter might read:

Thank you for your interest in employment with our firm.

While your qualifications are indeed excellent, they are not as closely allied to the job requirements as those of some other applicants we have recently interviewed.

For this reason we cannot further encourage your application at this time.

Sincerely yours,

A promptly written, tactful letter like this will not only keep rejected applicants from hounding you to find out their status, but will create as positive an image of your firm as is possible under the circumstances.

The top applicant should then be called in for a third meeting. He or she should be offered the job verbally and in writing. The other applicant should be kept waiting until the primary applicant formally accepts the position *and* reports to work.

Once the candidate has been offered a position with the company and has accepted, he or she should be required to take a medical examination at company expense. Then the owner or sales manager should sent the new employee a brief letter of confirmation. Here is an example:

We are pleased to confirm our offer to you and to learn that you will be joining us on Monday, September 13, 1982.

Your job duties are as outlined in the attached job description. You will be compensated at the rate of $1,500 a month in salary, payable the first and third Friday of each month, plus a commission of 1 percent of gross margin sales from all accounts in your territory. This commission will be paid by the third Friday of the month following shipment.

You and your family will be covered by our Blue Cross medical plan. Insurance and other benefits, including reimbursement of automobile and entertainment expenses, are in accordance with company policy currently in effect.

We are delighted to have you join us and trust that your employment with our organization will be mutually advantageous.

Sincerely,

Encl: Job Description
      Territory Map

SEARCHING FOR SALES REPS OR DISTRIBUTORS

Sales Reps

Referrals are the best way of finding qualified sales reps. Prospects and customers in the desired territory are already dealing with reps, and they can often recommend a good person to you. Follow up on this type of referral whenever you can, because when you engage the rep you usually get the prospect or customer as well. Sales reps, particularly those that now carry your line, can put you in touch with reps in other locations who handle similar lines. You might also try sales managers of noncompeting but similar lines who employ reps. Trade association executives and editors of trade publications may also be helpful.

Another good source is the Manufacturers' Agents National Association (MANA), which publishes an annual directory in July. This directory lists agents, product lines, and state headquarters. It costs $50. MANA is heavily oriented toward industry, but not exclusively so. It has member agents from just about every industry and type of trade, and it offers associate memberships to manufacturers. It can be reached by writing or calling the Manufacturers' Agents National Association, P.O. Box 16878, 2021 Business Center Drive, Irving, CA 92713; telephone (714) 752-5231.

You can also advertise in business publications such as *The Wall Street Journal* and the business section of the Sunday *New York Times*. For less ambitious searches, try the trade publications in your field and, of course, your local newspapers. Often your participation in trade shows will flush out reps looking for a new line. It's a good idea to keep a file of potential reps to contact when the need arises.

Idea #48: **"The time to look for people and for money is when you don't need them."** (Georges S. Doriot, my favorite professor at Harvard Business School.)

Other Sources

The National Council of Salesmen's Organizations, Inc. is located at Room 515, 225 Broadway, New York, NY 10007; telephone (212) 349-1707. It offers the names of trade organizations made up of reps in over 100 industries. The council also publishes a magazine, *Voice*.

Verified Directory of Manufacturers' Agents has an exclusive listing of all types of manufacturers' agents. This directory can be purchased from Manufacturers' Agents Publishing Co., 663 Fifth Avenue, New York, NY 10022; telephone (212) 682-0326.

In addition, your local sales executive club or chamber of commerce and the trade associations within your industry can often supply you with lists of agents.

If you are looking for specialty salespeople or agents, they can often be found by advertising in magazines such as *Income Opportunities*, 229 Park Avenue South, New York, NY 10003; telephone (212) 673-1300. Sometimes you can find the agents listed in the Yellow Pages of the telephone directories, under "Manufacturers' Agents and Representatives," for territories you want covered. For a fee, finders will help you determine the type of agents you need and will find them for you. There are a number of firms that provide this service. They include: Albee-Campbell, Inc., 578-580 Pennsylvania Avenue, Sinking Spring, PA 19608, and Anthony J. Zino Associates, 2 Park Avenue, Manhasset, NY 11030. Back Scratchers Club, Commerce Towers, Kansas City, MO 64105 offers a "lines and reps available" exchange for manufacturers and reps, as does Manufacturers' Agents Newsletter, Inc., 23573 Prospect Avenue, Farmington, MI 48024.

Reps are not hard to find, except for a few unusual product categories. Selecting the people right for you, however, can be difficult, and a careful study is called for. Once you become associated, you are as good as married. You can get a divorce, but it's often costly and painful, so don't rush into any relationship. Pick and choose carefully; the less often you have to change an agent in a territory, the better off you are.

Edwin Bobrow, in his excellent book on sales reps, has an

exemplary letter of appointment to a sales representative. (See Figure 6-2.)

Distributors

In your search for distributors, you can use some of the sources listed for sales representatives. The Yellow Pages are especially useful because distributors are listed for a given geographic area, and the major lines that they carry are often shown.

Finding a rep or distributor who will take on your product line is not hard at all, but finding one who will aggressively push your products is a different matter. The rep or distributor should have a good relationship with major prospects, yet not be so well established that he or she is content to coast with current lines and not push yours. It may be advisable for you to engage a rep who is already carrying two or three *major* lines, but not more than five or six.

COMPENSATION TECHNIQUES

Sales reps are compensated entirely on a commission basis. The only expenses that a sales rep receives from a manufacturer are for trips to the home office (for a sales meeting, for instance). The manufacturer usually picks up the tab for hotel and meals and splits or lets the rep pay the travel cost.

Compensation of direct salespersons is more complex. Payment arrangements run the gamut from straight salary to straight commission. To gain some perspective, let's look at the shifts in approaches that have taken place over the last 30 year.

In the late 1940s Professor Harry R. Tosdal and Walter O. Carlson of Harvard University conducted a sales compensation study. Two similar, more recent studies, one by Jack Davner and one by The American Management Associations, illustrate the shifts in compensation programs over time. The figures in Table 3 show that three-quarters of all sales compensation programs now include a combination salary and commission/bonus arrangement.

Figure 6-2. Sales rep appointment letter. (Source: Edwin E. Bobrow, *Marketing Through Manufacturers' Agents*, New York: Sales & Marketing Management, 1976, pp. 21–26. Reprinted by permission.)

XYZ CORPORATION
One Essex Place
Boston, MA 02213

Robert Greenshaw   January 4, 1982
Greenshaw and Associates
130 Memorial Drive
Milwaukee, Wisconsin 53205

Dear Mr. Greenshaw:

This will confirm our December 15, 1981 conversation that you are appointed as our representative for the states of Illinois and Wisconsin effective immediately.

It is understood that you are an independent, commissioned representative and in no way an agent or employee of the company and shall have no authority to bind or obligate the company.

It is further understood that this appointment is subject to cancellation by either party upon the giving to the other of notice in writing not less than sixty (60) days of intention to terminate and cancel and upon such stated date our agreement shall be thereafter void and of no force and effect.

The commission rates for all customers are as follows: 10 percent commission is paid on all accounts of 50/10 percent discounts (with the exception of 8 percent for Sears and 7 percent for Montgomery Ward) and a 5 percent commission is paid on all distributor accounts (that is, accounts with a discount of 50/10/20 percent). A service fee of 5 percent will be paid on all accounts serviced by you on a regular cycle of four to five weeks provided that your name appears on the reorders you write. (There is no service fee paid on distributor accounts). Any commission or service fee paid on sales which become uncollectable will be charged back to your account.

Commissions will be paid within 15 days of the end of the month for all goods shipped and billed within your assigned territory during that month.

Please indicate your concurrence and agreement with the foregoing by signing and returning to us the attached copy of this letter.

XYZ CORPORATION

By _____
                    President

The undersigned does hereby agree to the foregoing this

_____day of _____198_____.

_____
                  Representative

Table 3.   Sales compensation plans.

Type of Plan	Percentage Using Plan				Trend ‡
	1950 *	1970 †	1980 ‡	1981 ‡	
Straight salary	19.8	20.4	20.4	18.9	Stable
Salary plus commission and/or bonus	45.8	64.1	72.4	74.8	Expanding
Commission plan with guaranteed draw	10.7	4.0			
Commission plan without guaranteed draw	23.7	11.5	7.2	6.3	Declining
Total	100.0	100.0	100.0	100.0	

*Harry R. Tosdal and Walter O. Carlson, Jr., *Salesmen's Compensation* (Boston: Division of Research, Harvard University Graduate School of Business Administration, 1953).

†Jack R. Davner, *Salesmen's Compensation Plans, Policies and Trends* (Birmingham, MI: Sales Success Unlimited, February 1971).

‡American Management Associations, 1981/82 Executive Compensation Service *Sales Personnel Report*, 26th ed.

The growth in this approach has been at the expense of the draw-against-commission approach.

My own policy reflects this trend. I favor a compensation package of 75 percent salary and 25 percent commission. Such a ratio allows the salesperson to plan on a regular income, while still encouraging initiative.

The salary portion of the ratio should be adjusted annually in accordance with such prearranged evaluation factors as seniority, additional duties, and administrative effectiveness (such as turning in call plans and reports on time). The commission portion should be adjusted so as to pay 10 to 15 percent more in total compensation for expected results than if the salesperson were on a straight salary. This bonus compensates the salesperson for the risk inherent in any commission plan. As an example, suppose a sales manager projects sales for a territory at $500,000

Figure 6-3.   Salesperson's projected earnings.

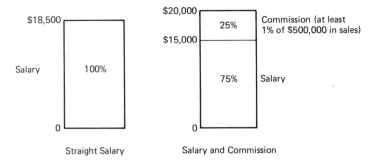

for the next year. (This projection is based on last year's sales, plus a planned inflationary price increase, plus a 10 percent normal sales growth.) If the salesperson for that territory would receive a straight salary of $18,500 annually, then using the above formula, a salesperson receiving salary plus commission would be paid $15,000 annually plus at least 1 percent commission. This is illustrated in Figure 6-3. Salary payments should be made biweekly, with commissions paid by the middle of the month after the one in which they were earned.

> **Idea #49:   The sooner a sales commission is paid after it has been earned, the more effective it is in motivating the salesperson.**

> **Idea #50:   To minimize strife within a sales force, keep the rate of commission the same for all the salespeople. Vary the salary to differentiate.**

A question often arises as to whether a rep or a salesperson whose earnings are partly or totally derived from commission should be asked to call on "house accounts," and be paid for doing so. House accounts are usually long-standing major customers who are visited primarily by the company's owner or sales manager. No standard answer can be given to this question, but my thoughts are:

1. House accounts should *never* exceed six to eight in number for a company with annual sales under $10,000,000.
2. The fewer the house accounts, the higher the sales morale.
3. Salespeople should receive some compensation for all accounts in their territory, regardless of when the account was opened and by whom. If the salesperson is expected to visit the house account infrequently then, perhaps, the base salary can provide that compensation. If frequent calls are to be made, then the salesperson should receive some extra compensation.

TERMINATING SALESPEOPLE

No discussion of hiring salespeople would be complete without coming to grips with the sad necessity of firing the ones who don't work out. Act promptly and decisively when a salesperson does not live up to your expectations. As owner or sales manager, you probably will form a judgment of an individual's potential within three months from the time he or she joins your firm. In 80 to 90 percent of the cases, your opinion will remain unchanged for the duration of the person's employment in your firm. So it's to everyone's advantage to act promptly.

> **Idea #51:   After three or more months, if you feel that a salesperson has been and will be unproductive, it's time to sever the connection—for the good of both the firm and the salesperson. No one wants to struggle along in a job for which he or she is clearly unsuited.**

This is not to say that you should be a "hatchet man" with no consideration for the individual and the reasons for his or her apparent failure. When a sales employee is not performing adequately (for example, not making enough prospect calls or total calls, giving poor demonstrations, and so on), try to pinpoint the trouble. Discuss your impressions candidly with the employee.

Try to help him or her improve performance by offering suggestions and encouragement.

If the problem persists, it's necessary to take the next step: Prepare a written warning to the employee, allowing for, say, a probationary period of a month in which the salesperson is obliged to do a better job. The employee should be required to countersign this probationary notice.

Idea #52:   When firing an employee, make certain that you have issued a written warning and that you can legally substantiate your actions.

It's a good policy to terminate an employee in a face-to-face meeting, not by telephone or letter. Experienced sales managers always make sure that the terminated employee has turned in all his or her company property, including customer lists and company car, *before* issuing the final paycheck.

Successful sales organizations cannot tolerate deadwood. Terminations are unpleasant for all concerned, but they should be regarded as a positive step in the program to increase your sales and achieve your marketing goals. The people on your staff are crucial to success, and so is the way you guide them and motivate them, as we will see in the next chapter.

CHAPTER 7

Getting the Most out of Your Selling Operation

Training, motivation, and control—these are the decisive elements in a successful selling operation. To get the most out of your sales efforts, you need to concentrate on all three.

TRAINING

Small and medium-size businesses often neglect training, reducing it to the infrequent demonstration of a new product. Even managers who profess to believe in training confine their efforts to the weekly sales meeting, and the main subject taught is usually product knowledge. There's little attempt to train salespeople in selling techniques. The attitude seems to be that a person brings selling skills to the job—or learns on the job. If the salesperson produces, fine. If not, he or she is ultimately terminated. It's that simple.

Obviously, this casual approach leaves much to be desired. A sound training program on an ongoing basis may seem time consuming and expensive, but in my experience it's essential to getting the most out of your selling operation. Don't train only weaker personnel; include the stars as well as the rookies. And as leader of the operation, you should be involved as well.

Training Begins with You

Idea #53: The most important person to be trained is the owner.

If you, the owner, don't continue to develop your personal resources, your shortcomings will limit the further expansion of your business. Your capabilities and vision shape your firm's destiny by setting the limits of growth. You need to enlarge your potential through training and education in order to accommodate growth by others on your sales staff. Owners who pursue self-education and who welcome new ideas run companies that grow much faster and go farther than those who do not. Curiously, such owners often have not received as much formal education as their counterparts in other companies. The recognition of their inadequate formal education probably spurs these owners on to fulfill their own potential. It's natural for others on the staff to follow the owner's lead. The result is a company with broadening horizons staffed by people with the know-how for achieving new goals.

How do you train yourself? There are many ways. Reading books like this one is a good start. There are hundreds available on every conceivable business subject. It's important to choose carefully, though, because many tend to be theoretical and academic, and are more suited to the classroom than to the office or plant. Instructional pamphlets put out by the Small Business Administration of the United Sates government are practical publications written with you in mind. They contain information pertinent to many areas of your business, and are especially helpful in presenting government regulations and describing business opportunities for products or services in specific geographic areas.

I believe that the best opportunities for personal growth come from participation in the many business seminars now available. These range from evening sessions lasting two hours to intensive two- or three-day programs like those sponsored by the American Management Associations and other professional groups. These seminars focus on specific areas of business knowledge in realistic and stimulating ways. There is enough variety among the seminars offered around the country to meet most educational needs. Look at the number and variety of the courses recently listed by the American Management Associations in a single catalog:

Number of Courses	Topic Area
44	Sales and Marketing
36	Finance
35	Information Systems and Technology
35	Manufacturing
31	Human Resources
27	Technology Management
25	General Management
20	Insurance and Employee Benefits
18	Purchasing, Transportation, Distribution

Business schools and regional business associations around the country offer similar seminars and short courses designed to meet the needs of small businesses. For example, the major event of the Smaller Business Association of New England (SBANE) is a half-week session at Dartmouth's Amos Tuck School of Business. SBANE also holds a series of one-day seminars, which have proved immensely popular among New England business people. There are similar programs sponsored by business groups all over the country.

The value of such programs goes beyond classroom instruction, important as that might be. Seminar organizers are aware that participants are experienced businessmen well able to contribute to the educational process. There is always plenty of time for discussing and exchanging ideas with people of similar interests and problems, and this is one of the most valuable aspects of such seminars. Informal discussions in the classroom as well as bull sessions in dining room and bar can provide many good ideas that you can bring back to your office and put to work for your company. If you leave a seminar with just one very good idea, it's probably been worth your investment of time and money.

Idea #54: A business person should try to spend a minimum of half a day a week learning something new.

Of course, your "training" need not come from books or formal education. Having lunch with the president of another company may prove more useful than a dozen lectures. And you can learn about ways to improve your operations by visiting trade shows, showrooms, and the like to see demonstrations of new products or listen to ideas about new services. Ideally, your openness to learning experiences should carry over to the staff, and you can help to make this happen by establishing an ongoing program based on your goals for the company.

Training Your Staff

Idea #55: If salespeople are to improve their performance, they must be encouraged to do so. It's a rare person who will seek improvement in job skills on his or her own initiative.

The object of your training program for marketing people should be to improve knowledge of the products they sell and skill in the way they sell them.

Sales Techniques

Here are three approaches for helping your sales staff develop the selling skills they need:

1. *Outside sales training courses.* Dale Carnegie offers an inexpensive 12-week course on selling techniques that is practical and very effective if the instructor is capable. The course meets one night a week and is available in major cities. I gained more practical knowledge from this course than from any at Harvard Business School, and I heartily recommend it! Another superior opportunity available in major cities is a shorter (two-and-a-half-day) program in selling techniques under the auspices of Xerox Learning Systems.

2. *Sales trainers.* Many small businesses engage inspiring sales trainers to talk to their salespeople for a day or two each year. This works very well for one of my clients, ENSACO, whose salespeople are engineering oriented. They benefit from the emphasis on the arts of persuasion and human relations that sales trainers usually stress. Of course, selling requires far more than inspiration; there are many empirical techniques involved, as we saw in Chapter 4. Sales trainers can help the veterans on your staff as well as the novices, because they can offer insights into the arts of selling that are often overlooked or ignored.

The best way of finding capable trainers is through referrals— from customers, business associates, and friends, for example. Another source is the Yellow Pages under the heading "Sales Training." You might also try your local marketing groups, such as Sales & Marketing Executives and the American Marketing Association.

3. *Role playing.* This approach is excellent for sales meetings, but it does require some preparation. Start by providing one of your senior sales representatives with background material on an actual or sample sales situation. Have this representative then assume the role of the purchasing agent or engineer.

Ask a volunteer from the sales force to make a sales call on this "purchasing agent" or "engineer." (If no one volunteers, choose someone whose selling talents are known to you.) The sales presentation should be done in front of the entire sales staff. After the call has been completed, encourage staff members to provide comments and suggestions.

Be sure that there is enough time for at least two sales situations to be presented at the same meeting. This lessens the pressure on the people who do the role playing simply because they share the spotlight with their peers. Role playing can be an effective way for salespeople to improve their techniques, correct errors, and generally learn more about themselves and their effect on customers. But it also can be stressful for some to get up in front of an audience and perform. For this reason, don't expect too much from your first two or three sessions. It usually takes that long before your salespeople feel comfortable with role playing. In my experience, role playing can be a useful training technique, but it is no panacea. Some owners never feel comfortable with it, others find it is appropriate only for new salespeople, and still others find it requires too much preparation. Nonetheless, role playing as a sales training technique deserves your serious consideration, simply because it's the only technique readily available. Remember, such training has only one purpose: to improve the effectiveness of your sales force.

All the elements of sales effectiveness are probably never found in one individual. Every salesperson has strengths and weaknesses. When you select topics for your sales training sessions, it's helpful to be aware of the qualities that buyers value most in the salespeople they deal with. The results of a *Sales & Marketing Management* survey (see Figure 7-1) can offer some insights.

Products
Teaching people what they need to know about your products is usually simpler and more straightforward than training them in the techniques of selling. This is not to minimize its importance. A salesperson can't possibly be effective without a thorough knowledge of the products he or she tries to sell. In small businesses, one way to insure that salespeople know the product is to hire only those with experience with similar products in the same industry. Another is to give new employees positions inside the company (in customer service, for instance) for an indoctrination period of a year or two. If an experienced salesperson is unfamiliar with the products of his or her new employer or the markets to be served, that person should spend some time in the home office to learn about the product before going out into the field. Usually this period need not last more than a month. After that, the new salesperson can gain further knowledge of the product through regular sales meetings and on-the-job experience.

Many small businesses can't afford elaborate training programs, but they can and should emphasize product education at the weekly or monthly sales meetings. In most situations the best approach is to have one of your senior salespeople lead a discussion for your sales staff in which the product is described or demonstrated. Besides improving the junior sales staff's under-

Figure 7-1. Qualities that make salespeople tops. (Source: "Qualities That Make Salespeople Tops," *Sales keting Management*, August 20, 1979, p. 38. ©1979. Reprinted by permission.)

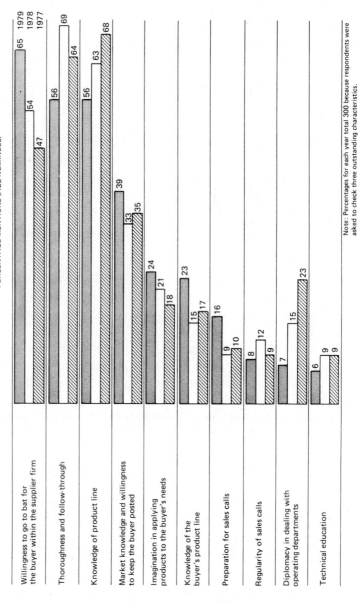

PERCENTAGE MENTIONS (ALL NOMINEES)

Quality	1979	1978	1977
Willingness to go to bat for the buyer within the supplier firm	65	54	47
Thoroughness and follow-through	56	69	64
Knowledge of product line	56	63	68
Market knowledge and willingness to keep the buyer posted	39	33	35
Imagination in applying products to the buyer's needs	24	21	18
Knowledge of the buyer's product line	23	15	17
Preparation for sales calls	16	9	10
Regularity of sales calls	8	12	9
Diplomacy in dealing with operating departments	7	15	23
Technical education	6	9	9

Note: Percentages for each year total 300 because respondents were asked to check three outstanding characteristics.

standing of your product line, this approach gives the senior salesperson some training in planning and conducting a presentation (training that is important for a future management position), and it increases the speaker's own knowledge of the product line.

Salespeople for distributors have much more to learn about many more different products than most other sales personnel. If you run a distributorship, it's a good idea to have the manufacturers whose lines you carry instruct your sales employees about the advantages of their products over their competitors' through sales meetings and joint sales calls. One sales meeting a month should be devoted to product characteristics and should include instruction by a representative of one of the manufacturers you represent.

MOTIVATION

Idea #56: The key to sales motivation is management's attention and support.

"Attention" refers to your interest in the sales force and in the problems and performance of its individual members. "Support" refers to the compensation program and the tools of sales support, which we discuss at greater length in Chapter 8.

Idea #57: The extent of your involvement in the selling function usually influences the morale and performance of sales representatives.

Recently one of my clients, who prides himself on having the highest paid and most effective distributors' sales force in his industry in New England, came to me with the problem of declining morale. One of his top salesmen had resigned and others had expressed concern that they were being treated "like second-class citizens."

The situation arose because a year earlier the owner had promoted one of his salesmen to the position of sales manager. He
wanted to free himself from the day-to-day sales problems and,
at the same time, provide more professional training, support, and
control for his field personnel. But the salesmen resented this
move; they felt they were being downgraded, and had been for-
gotten by the owner. The new sales manager didn't help the situation. Rather than balancing himself between the sales force and
the owner, he allied himself totally with the owner. He moved
into an office in headquarters and rarely went out into the field
with the men.

I reminded the owner that selling is a lonely profession. The
salesperson, cut off from the warmth of the home office, is in
constant conflict with the buyer. One tries to sell, the other to
resist. Under these circumstances, the salespeople felt they lost
their best friend when the owner appointed the sales manager.
They needed an authority figure in the home office in whom they
had confidence and trust. To correct the situation, the owner had
to pay more attention to his salespeople as individuals and needed
to show that he understood their problems and valued their work.
In time, he found another, more field-oriented sales manager who
works closely with the salespeople. The first sales manager has
now become the manager of sales administration.

That kind of attention and concern is especially needed when
dealing with independent sales reps. Reps are entrepreneurs who
run their own businesses, but they're not always businesslike.
They want your encouragement and support if they are to push
your products. A rep who knows you personally and likes the
way you do business will often sell your product in favor of your
competitors', even when it may not offer as much income
potential.

**Idea #58: The objective in dealing with sales reps should
be to get them to invest a disproportionately large amount
of time on your line in relation to the amount of income
they can expect in return.**

The way to achieve an added investment of time and effort on the part of sales reps is simply by giving them *attention* and *support*. Communicate often with the rep and take an interest in his or her problems. Supply sales leads, product literature, and prompt response to field problems and requests for expedited deliveries.

A generous financial reward is usually one of the more effective "carrots." Your "stick" as far as reps are concerned is the possibility that you will take your line away and give it to another rep. This may or may not have the intended effect, depending on how much income your products generate for the rep. As a matter of fact, the stick approach to motivation works best with direct salespeople, and only then when it is heavily outweighed by carrots! Personally, I prefer a 75 percent to 25 percent ration of reward to punishment as a method of non-monetary motivation.

In a recent report to one of my clients, I recommended the following motivational strategies, which should be valid for most direct sales forces.

Positive—three "carrot" motivators:

- Define responsibilities. Provide an up-to-date and accurate job description and regular performance reviews.
- Provide a voice for the field salespeople in establishing their own quotas.
- Set up a simple, easy-to-understand compensation plan that rewards people according to their performance.

Negative—two "stick" motivators:

- If a sales representative fails to penetrate a major account within a reasonable period of time (six months to a year) in accordance with its potential, transfer that account to another salesperson's territory.
- If a salesperson fails to meet an agreed-upon sales or profit quota, transfer him or her to a new territory or terminate employment.

There are numerous other methods for motivating sales-people, including peer pressure. This approach works in a firm that employs between 6 and 25 salespeople and has an equitable method for allocating territories and potential. For each sales period, the sales manager posts the names of all the salespeople and each one's sales performance. This is a neat carrot-and-stick combination—a carrot for those at the top, a stick for those at the bottom.

I know a large New England automobile dealer who follows this plan, with just one change. He fires the person at the bottom of the list every month! Perhaps such Draconian measures work for that particular dealer, but please be cautious about following his lead. Working under such pressure must be stultifying for all salespeople. They can't give their best in these conditions. There are far more reasonable motivators.

Take, for instance, the "peer competition program" instituted by Van Phillips, president of Markoa Corporation and former president of Sales Marketing Executives of Chicago. Under the Phillips plan, every salesperson receives a low "living requirement" base salary. Then each week the person also gets a certain number of points, determined by the gain over a base-point total and by productivity. The points are translated quarterly or semi-annually into a bonus paid out of a common pool. The best salespeople receive a higher percentage of the pool, and often take home six times as much as their less effective associates. Phillips says that the peer competition program is by far the most productive of any program he has tried. Table 4 shows how it worked out one year for six salespeople.

CONTROL

If you are to maintain tight control over an individual, you must be involved closely with that person, have his or her undivided attention, and be able to exercise a valid system of rewards and punishments. It is very difficult for a manufacturer to have that type of involvement with sales reps and distributor personnel, but one technique that I have recently observed is worth noting.

Table 4. Results of Van Phillips' peer competition program.

Sales person	Annual Base Salary	Bonus Points Paid Quarterly	Value of Bonus Point	Total Annual Income
R. Anderson	$17,000	74	$200	$31,800
L. Cleavley	10,000	62	$200	22,400
J. Farnsworth	11,000	46	$200	20,200
I. Leavitt	12,500	80	$200	28,500
B. Nesbitt	8,500	42	$200	16,900
W. Ray	12,000	50	$200	22,000

(Source: *Portfolio of 1977 Sales & Marketing Plans*, New York: Sales & Marketing Management, 1977, pp. 41–42. Reprinted by permission.)

Stayflex, a New York manufacturer of nonwoven apparel materials, places its own direct salespeople in the offices of its major distributors. Each salesperson is thus available to the distributor's sales force to make joint calls, assist in technical support, and expedite requests for special orders. At the same time, you can bet that this person is also influencing the distributor's sales force in favor of Stayflex products.

Stayflex has devised an unusual method of exerting control over the way its products are sold by distributors. Most manufacturers and distributors try to control selling operations solely by concentrating their efforts on the direct sales force.

Idea #59: A basic control system can be constructed by requiring three types of reports: a weekly call report, a corporate call report, and a monthly hot-prospect report.

The Weekly Call Report

The weekly call report (WCR) is the backbone of any sales control system. While the format may vary, the WCR should include certain basic elements. Take a look at the sample WCR shown in Figure 7-2, which includes a section for expense reim-

Figure 7-2. Weekly call report.

FIELD SALES REP. _____ WEEK ENDING _____				

Day	Company and City	Prospect (P) or Customer(C)	Date Call Completed	Comments
Mon.				
Tues.				
Wed.				
Thurs.				
Fri.				

EXPENSES: ENTERTAINMENT

Date	Company—Guests	Position	City	Type of Entertainment	Cost

Automobile   Mileage _____ X ____ ¢ mile = _____

Telephone _____   Tolls & Parking _____   Other _____ = _____

Approved _____   _____ Total

bursement. Under this arrangement the sales manager tells the salesperson, in effect: "No call report, no expense reimbursement."

Idea #60: Want to make sure that your sales staff submits the weekly call report on time? Combine the report with the tabulation of expenses incurred.

The WCR serves as both a planning document and a call report document. It should be completed in triplicate, using carbon paper. The Sunday before the week covered by the report, the salesperson should fill in the "Company and City" and "Prospect or Customer" columns as a list of the visits he or she *plans* to make that week. One copy of this call plan is submitted to the sales manager on Monday, early in the morning if possible.

During the week, the salesperson fills out the last two columns of the form as the visits are actually completed, also writing in expenses incurred and any changes in plans—for example, postponed or canceled visits. The second copy of the WCR is submitted the following Monday, so that the sales manager can compare plans with actual results. The third copy is retained by the salesperson.

It's a good idea to rank the importance of your customer accounts with an alphabetic or numeric designation. This allows the sales manager to assess coverage of accounts in relation to your established priorities.

Idea #61: Pay close attention to WCRs! If they are to have any value, they must be submitted on time and on a regular basis. And they must be read and acknowledged by the sales manager.

You, the owner, should pay attention to WCRs as well. Read them at least occasionally to keep abreast of what your sales staff is doing. This is one way to give salespeople the attention and support necessary to get the most from them.

The Corporate Call Report

The corporate call report (CCR) is designed to be used both as a company record of all calls on a particular account and as a quick update on information about the account for the salesperson. (Accounts can be either customers or prospects.) Furthermore, the CCR becomes a control tool for the sales manager in monitoring a sales employee's coverage of an account.

Idea #62: When a salesperson leaves your company, the CCR provides you with a complete record of each customer and prospect account visited.

The CCR should contain, on the front page, the background data on the firm, including the names of key personnel and all possible product applications. See the sample in Figure 7-3(a). The back page is used to log the dates when visits were made and any comments, as shown in Figure 7-3(b).

CCRs should be kept together in a loose-leaf notebook, clearly labelled as being the property of your company. It should have an inventory serial number and be signed out to the salesperson covering that territory. Whenever the owner or sales manager is inquiring about an account or making joint calls with the salesperson on that account, he or she should be sure to see the CCR book.

Some firms also use an individual call report. Under this system the salesperson writes up, on a printed form, the results of each call. I believe that such a report can be helpful to document a specific problem or competitive situation, but if used for every call it burdens the salesperson with excess paperwork. However, for salespeople in particularly remote areas, an employer may seek control by requiring individual call reports for every call.

Monthly Hot-Prospect Report

Another report, particularly helpful for capital equipment or major new account selling, is the monthly hot-prospect report,

Figure 7-3(a). Corporate call report—front.

PACIFIC STEEL CO., INC.
Spokane, Washington

Date _____

Company _____

Address _____ Phone _____

City _____ State _____

Warehouse buyer _____ Mill buyer _____

Product Manufactured (If job shop, state as much)

_____

_____

_____

_____

Type of Market

    Type of Steel Used   Where Used

_____   _____

_____   _____

_____   _____

_____   _____

_____   _____

_____   _____

COMMENTS

_____

_____

_____

_____

Figure 7-3(b).   Corporate call report—back.

Date Visited	Comments	Date Visited	Comments

shown in Figure 7-4. It has been my experience that the average capital equipment salesperson will list between four and twelve prospects and will ultimately close one or two each month.

If the same firm's name appears for three consecutive months on this list, then the sales manager should try to assist the salesperson by helping decide what action should be taken to obtain the order from that account.

Figure 7-4.   Monthly hot-prospect report.

List only prospects you feel will definitely close.

Salesperson_____ Territory _____ Month _____

Prospect Firm	City/Town	Dates of Demo/Proposal	Comments

THE OVERALL PROGRAM

To get the most from your selling operation, you need to coordinate the three decisive elements—training, motivation, and control—in a way that your people understand and enthusiastically accept. Success in a selling operation usually follows when you can incorporate and act on these elements: Well-trained people tend to be well motivated; well-motivated people tend to follow your guidance and direction. There is a gung-ho spirit among successful salespeople that creates it's own atmosphere for further growth. You can enhance that atmosphere by means of your administrative skill and your support, as we shall see in the next chapter.

CHAPTER 8

Supporting Your Selling Program Through Advertising

Strong support from the home office constitutes the backbone of any selling operation. Without it, your salespeople in the field are weakened, a circumstance that usually manifests itself in reduced productivity and lowered morale.

What does "support" mean? It means, for one thing, generating sales leads for your field people. It also means supplying them with effective selling tools—user-oriented literature, and adequate quantities of product samples. Finally, support means instituting intelligent customer relations that include after-sale services such as prompt order processing and shipping and responsive repair/maintenance procedures.

THE IMPORTANCE OF SALES LEADS

Your survival as a company probably depends on the generation of new business. It is not just a matter of growth. Most companies need to acquire new customers every year just to stay even. This was pointed out to me a few years ago by Philip Warren, president of Paragon Steel Corporation of Detroit, Michigan. He said, "We experience a 14 percent attrition in our accounts each year. We lose one out of seven through no fault of our own. They go out of business or move away." I have found this phenomenon to be true of most of my clients.

Idea #63: In budgeting to increase your annual sales, remember that you won't be starting from your current sales level, but at a point 10 to 15 percent below that level. The reason: an inevitable attrition of your customer base.

Basically, there are two ways to generate the leads that result in new business:

1. *Helping the prospect find you.* This is a shotgun approach that brings your product or service to the attention of the prospective buyer. You can only hope that happens at a time when he or she needs your product or service.
2. *Helping your firm find the prospect.* This is a rifle approach that places you in contact with firms that have a need for your product, but are currently using some other.

Which course is right for you? Fortunately, it's not an either/or proposition. You should use both the shotgun and rifle approaches simultaneously.

HELPING THE PROSPECT FIND YOU

To help a potential customer find your company, you must advertise in the right places. More than anything else, the effectiveness of your promotional program depends on the media you choose. Here are the prime outlets for advertising your products or services.

Yellow Pages

Almost every business can benefit from advertising in the Yellow Pages of the telephone directory. The reason is that so many buyers turn to this medium when searching out a new supplier. How can you get the best results from Yellow Pages advertising? Here are a few tips given to me by Robert Caswell, directory sales manager of New England Telephone Company.

A Yellow Pages reader typically starts at the beginning of a section and reads from that point on, stopping at the first firm that meets his or her selection criteria. The reader tries to ascertain whether a particular outfit can do the job and whether it is reliable.

There are two basic kinds of ads in the Yellow Pages. The cheaper ones are the informational listings, colloquially called "business cards." These are small and usually enclosed in a plain box with the company's name at the top, and they are alphabetized right in with the regular listings of names and addresses only.

More expensive are the display ads. These are the ones with fancy borders, boldface type, and pictures. In telephone directories of small cities and in some of the new *Business to Business* directories for large cities, display ads are listed alphabetically by size. Space is sold in quarter-column units. The largest ads (each using *four* quarter-column units) come first, in alphabetical order. These are followed by the next largest ads, in alphabetical order, each using *three* quarter-column units. Then come the *two*-unit and the *one*-unit ads.

However, in some large cities such as Boston and Providence, the telephone company gives priority to former advertising subscribers when positioning ads. Thus a new advertiser can obtain more impact in a small-city directory, where seniority is not a consideration. (This is particularly true for firms whose names come near the beginning of the alphabet.)

There are other ways to call attention to your ad besides being listed near the beginning of your category. An attractive layout can catch the reader's eye, and in some cities the telephone company is beginning to offer ads in color. Before you place an ad, be sure to discuss all your options thoroughly with your Yellow Pages representative.

All ads, to be effective, should contain the following components in bold print:

- A lead-in discribing the specific service offered. Don't depend on the page or section heading. Say what you offer loud and clear. "WE CLEAN CARPETS," "I SELL LAWN MOWERS."
- Your firm's name, inserted in the middle of the body copy.
- Your firm's telephone number, at the end of the ad. This should be the action step for the customer. Print it in boldface type.

Thomas Register

The *Thomas Register* is an important advertising vehicle as well as market research tool (see Chapter 2). The *Register* catalogs the products and services of all firms in the United States. More than 95,000 are listed alphabetically by category and by a product index, subdivided first by state, then by city within state, and finally by company within city.

Custom manufacturers (job shops) in particular should invest sufficient funds in a *Thomas Register* ad to assure effective presentation of their capabilities. Follow the tips suggested for advertising in the Yellow Pages.

Other Directories

Two other types of directories provide vehicles for advertising your product or service: Product/service directories are usually produced by trade associations. They list members and include some advertising. Their value as a source of sales leads is limited to OEM or service suppliers searching out sales prospects among organization members.

Geographical directories are available on a state or regional basis. They list manufacturers both by state and town and by SIC category. The listing usually includes the address and telephone number of each company, the number of employees, the names of the executive officers, and a short description of products or services.

Other Publications

Supplemental sources of advertising include local business publications. Check your region to see what is available. Most parts of the country have newspapers or newsletters devoted to business that cover major events, company moves, personnel changes, and new product introductions. There are also magazines published by state business associations or commercial publishers. Magazine advertising tends to be expensive when measured against average response. *New England Business,* a well-written, semi-monthly magazine in my area, recently increased responses to its ads by the introduction of a reader reply card. Such regional publications are worth considering for inclusion in your advertising plans because they reach a fair number of potential customers within your area. Test the effectiveness of regional business publications by running an ad three or four times and noting the response.

New Product Releases

New product releases can boost your selling program and should be used whenever the opportunity arises. They are treated as news by newspapers and trade magazines, so there is no charge for their publication. Editors, particularly those of trade publications, are happy to print them in the "new products" column, which is the best-read section of every trade magazine.

Writing a new product release is not difficult, but to give your release the best chance of publication, you should observe certain professional rules of the road. Stick to the facts. Keep your sales pitch to a minimum and follow the standard 5W formula: include information about who, what, where, when, and why in the first paragraph, and then provide further details in succeeding paragraphs. Use standard newspaper format. Put a factual headline on the first page, and start the story halfway down on page one. Include the name and telephone number of someone in your company whom the editor can call for further information. A sample news release is illustrated in Figure 8-1. Be sure to include a glossy 8 in. by 10 in. photograph.

Of course, your advertising agency will be glad to prepare your new product releases for a fee. The agency will also take care of the mailing, making sure that copies get to all the publications important in your industry among your customers and prospects.

Figure 8-1.   Sample news release for a new product. (Courtesy WB Inc.)

```
                    RUGGED SELF-STANDING MANUAL LIFT

                    SAFELY RAISES 1,500 LBS 24 FT
```

A new, low-cost, hand-operated lift that can be used alone or with two or more lifts for a variety of installation, maintenance, and construction applications is being introduced by WB Incorporated of Boston, Massachusetts.

The WB Inc. Stabil-Lift safely raises 1,500 lbs, plus a live superimposed load, up to 24 ft high. Self-standing on a stable, 58½ in. by 93½ in. steel base, the winch-operated lift comes in 2- and 4-ft sections that are easily assembled in the field. Rated with a safety factor of 4, the column truss is designed to become more stable as weight increases.

Operated by a manual spur gear winch with a self-locking brake, the WB Inc. Stabil-Lift is made of rugged, steel alloy tubing in a 15 in. triangular frame. It features two 24 in. L lifting arms with accessories for lifting personnel, and has leveling screws for uneven terrain. Caster mounting is optional.

The WB Inc. Stabil-Lift is priced at $2,500, with 3 week delivery. Literature is available on request.

For more information contact: [name and address of company and representative]

News releases have unquestioned advantages over other promotional efforts. Not only are they published free of charge, they also have high credibility because they appear as text, not advertising. Product releases generally get an excellent response from readers. There are just two minor drawbacks—you can't be sure the magazine will print your release (although it helps if you are or have been an advertiser) and you have no control over the final copy; the release may be edited and rewritten, possibly losing accuracy and probably losing promotional thrust thereby.

Trade Shows

Trade shows are great for exposing your products and services to buyers and the interested public. Don't forget: they're a place to sell, not just advertise, as Al Hanlon emphasizes in his book, *Trade Shows in the Marketing Mix* (Boston: Herman Publishing, 1980).

Idea #64: Use trade show exhibits to generate sales leads. Trade shows can be an effective selling medium if you emphasize sales, rather than advertising, in your exhibit's approach.

Getting valid leads from a trade show is a science that includes such elements as:

- Pre-show mailings to prospects suggesting that they seek out your booth.
- An exhibit designed to attract prospect.
- An *in-motion* demonstration of your product.
- Specially trained and highly motivated booth sales personnel.
- Use of a hospitality suite.

Take a tip from Al Hanlon: Remember that your exhibit is not for advertising but for selling. You can generate strong new sales leads by designing your trade show participation with this concept in mind.

Set specific objectives for your trade show participation, just as you would for any sales program, and measure results. Figure 8-2 shows a good example from the Berlyn Corporation in Worcester, Massachusetts, manufacturers of machinery for the plastics industry.

FINDING THE PROSPECT

What about customers that have not expressed an interest in your product or service? Pursuing these can be challenging and rewarding. The challenge arises from the complexities of identifying and getting a response from your prospects, and then screening them. The reward is, of course, receiving their order for your merchandise. Such new customers are usually profitable because

Figure 8-2. Sample trade show objectives. (Courtesy Berlyn Corporation.)

TRADE SHOW OBJECTIVES	IMMEDIATE RESULTS
1. $100,000 in sales with purchase order numbers.	$71,550
2. 1,000 primary leads with qualifications.	544
3. 1,000 secondary leads.	231
4. We want to establish a big image.	Yes
5. We are introducing 4 new machines:	
Continuous filter	Success
Extruder	Neutral
Calcinator	Neutral
Densifier	Failure

Comments
   The continuous filter was a success. We learned that we did not belong in the densifier business. We did our market survey and made our design mistakes on the calcinator. We were too timid in the extruder business: we tried to back in without stepping on toes, and you can't do this. Today we're ready to take them *all* on in the extruder business!
   We converted an additional $208,450 directly into sales within three months of the show, and all that's for $35,055 spent on the trade show.

you may be able to avoid giving them discounts or special terms. Your only competition is likely to be their present supplier.

Identifying Suspects

A "suspect" is an unqualified prospect—that is, one about whom you know nothing yet. (To "qualify" sales leads means to find out exactly what they need and how likely they are to purchase your product. The second objective in Figure 8-2, for example, was to find sales leads *with* qualifications.) Ways of qualifying suspects will be discussed in detail a little later—but before you can qualify them, you have to find them.

The first step in finding suspects is to establish a search profile in which types and sizes of likely customers are selected, along with their geographic location and notes on their buying procedures. For instance, who is the decision maker? Who else influences the decision?

It's a simple enough task to identify suspects once you have chosen the particular market population likely to respond to what you have to sell. Here's how it worked for Sjogren Tool and Machine Company of Auburn, Massachusetts, a client of mine that saw an opportunity in sharpening and replacing industrial knife blades used on wire reclamation machines. Our problem was that we didn't know where the potential users of this service were located because Sjogren didn't build or sell reclamation machinery.

To develop a profile of suspects, I took 25 names from President Dick Sjogren's Christmas gift list of current blade accounts (I would normally use a customer list but in this case the Christmas list was more selective), and I then determined their four-digit SIC code. I used Dun and Bradstreet's *Million Dollar Directory* (see Chapter 2), and came up with 17 four-digit categories. Then I contacted representative firms in each category to determine how they used blades and whether or not they were a potential market for sharpening and replacement.

This was a winnowing process that ultimately led me to select three SIC categories that offered the greatest potential. For the geographic areas in which Sjogren had rep coverage we ordered sales lead cards from Dun & Bradstreet for all firms on the list with sales above a certain level. We sent out a mailing to both purchasing agents and maintenance engineers. Later we did a follow-up mailing. The results were forwarded to the reps. Sjogren was in the business of sharpening steel blades.

Screening Suspects by Phone

Once you have a suspect population, the next step is to identify the prospects among them—those, that is, that have an interest or potential interest in buying your products or services. You can do this by phone or letter.

The telephone approach is gaining increased acceptance because it is relatively inexpensive. Many small companies are succeeding with American Telephone & Telegraph's new Direct Marketing and Response System (DMARS). Telemarketing is being used more and more to set up appointments, sell small accounts, conduct seasonal selling, qualify sales leads, solicit renewals and repeat business, provide customer service, and collect overdue accounts.

Screening Suspects by Direct Mail

At one time or another, most business owners try their hand at writing their own direct mail letters.

Idea #65: Don't overlook the rich possibilities of direct mail for generating new sales leads. An effective and regularly repeated direct mail program probably provides the most practical method of finding prospects.

If your own letters don't evoke the response you expected, don't abandon direct mail altogether. Owners who turn to professionals for guidance often have much greater success. Back in 1970, I started writing my own direct mail letters as part of a campaign for generating sales leads. When I turned to professionals for assistance, direct mail became the backbone of my business through

1978. By that time, my referrals were sufficient in number that direct mail was no longer necessary as a prospecting medium.

There are three elements in any direct mail campaign for uncovering sales leads:

1. The mailing list.
2. The letter itself plus the reply vehicle.
3. The implementation of the mailing.

Idea #66:   Pay attention to these three elements in equal measure. Slighting of just one will usually undermine your direct mail campaign.

Let's examine each element with an eye toward better understanding of direct mail techniques.

Your Mailing List

The starting point is always the list of people and/or firms who are to be the recipients of the mailing. If you mail to people who are not prospects, obviously your mailing will be ineffective. Where do you get the names? Assuming you know your target audience by business category, you'll have no trouble getting professional help in finding names. A reputable list broker can provide a wondrous array of prospects for about $50.00 per one thousand names. A good list compiler, like Zeller-Lettica in New York, offers six million businesses and addresses, ranging from ice cream manufacturers (688 by count) to truck body dealers (2,022).

Some good advice about choosing your mailing list is found in the excellent booklet titled *Direct Mail*, published and distributed free of charge by the S. D. Warren Company of Boston, a division of Scott Paper Company. Here's an excerpt:

If you make a terrible mistake in direct mail, it will probably be in the way you handle mailing lists. Nothing is more important. Nothing is so often botched up. If you're casual about it, nothing will save you. The best copy and graphics in the world won't sell bottlecaps to a tuna cannery.

In choosing a list to mail to, the idea is to maximize the number of hot prospects and minimize the number of cold ones. List *narrowing* is as important as list building.

Let's say, for example, that you're in the business of selling snowshoes to police departments. Here are several possible lists.

- U.S. police departments.
- Equipment purchasers in U.S. police departments.
- Equipment purchasers in U.S. police departments *located in cold climates.*
- Equipment purchasers in *rural* U.S. police departments located in cold climates.

Each one of these categories is narrower and better than the one before it. But the best one of all would be something like this: equipment purchasers in U.S. police departments *who purchased snowshoes last year.* That's the list you should find.

It stands to reason that the best mailing list you'll ever get your hands on is what professionals call your house list: your present customers. They've all bought before. Most of them will buy again. You should also include the names of hot prospects that have been turned up by your salesmen and distributors. . . . Start with your house list. Then build, buy or rent.

The normal procedure (in dealing with a commercial list house) is to start with a catalog of lists, find the list that is closest to what you're looking for, and then have the computer extract specific names according to your specifications—sorting out by geographic area, industrial category, company size, personnel title, and so on.

By the way, some professionals feel that addressing a mailing to a title is more efficient than addressing to a name. The reason is obvious: titles are more permanent than the men or women who bear them.

A reputable list house will guarantee 95 percent deliverability on its mailing lists. You can expect some "moved" or "wrong address" returns by the Post Office, but they should represent a small percentage of your mailing.

Idea #67: Narrow your list so that it focuses on your target audience of prospects and mail to a specific title or name in that group. It costs more, but it's worth it!

Your letter

Your objective is simply to induce your prospect to raise his or her hand and say, "Yes, I'm interested!" Too much information in your letter confuses and bores the reader.

Idea #68: Avoid including too much information. The purpose of direct mail is to generate a sales lead, not to provide material for the recipient's product literature file.

The art of direct mail consists in piquing your prospect's interest enough to respond. The best way to do this, according to the experts, is to offer your reader something in return for his or her response. Don't ask the recipient to "check the box if interested and a salesperson will call." That doesn't work too well. Instead, make an offer—a how-to booklet, for instance, or a case history, or product literature. Such offers can be expected to produce a 1 to 10 percent response rate. You will be lucky to get a $1/_2$ percent response with hard-sell, "have our salesperson call" letters.

The names you get in response are valuable. A salesperson can follow them up by telephone or in person and can mail or deliver the offered item, depending on the prospect's qualifications. Don't think of the people as one-time buyers. They can be approached time and again.

The best response rate comes from "gimmick" letters of various kinds, which can yield 25 percent or higher. Gimmicks are offers designed to catch the reader's attention in an unusual way and to prompt him or her to respond. Two gimmicks that have been particularly effective for my clients are:

1. *The questionnaire.* Printed on blue legal-size paper, this format looks like a questionnaire but is, in reality, a selling piece. To complete the questionnaire the respondent must read the questions, all of which are sales "thought provokers."
2. *Money for your child's piggy bank.* It used to be a quarter. Now it's the Susan Anthony dollar coin that is sent with the mailing piece as a financial inducement to motivate the recipient to reply.

My opinion about gimmick letters is that for surveys and mailings, where a high rate of response is important, they are of value. But for the sales lead, where the quality of response is important, an offer works best.

One helpful technique in increasing responses and lowering printing costs is to have the transmittal letter double as the reply letter. By folding the transmittal letter into an "S" format, the name and address of the intended recipient can be positioned to show through the window of the envelope. Thus no address need be printed. And if you use a window envelope to make the letter look like a bill, people will open it. One typing provides you with the mailing address and, when the response is returned, the name of the respondee. The recipient is instructed to simply sign his or her name on the bottom of the letter, if interested, insert it in an enclosed postage-paid envelope, and return to the sender.

An automatically typed, personalized letter provides the most professional approach and produces the best response rate. In such a letter the recipient's name and address are individually typed. Then a button is pushed by the typist and the balance of the letter is typed automatically. Figure 8-3 is an example of such a letter. The use of relatively low-priced word processing machines has increased the popularity of this approach.

Similar to the above but less expensive is the matched fill-in

Figure 8-3.   Sample of an automatically typed, personalized gimmick letter.

Grayson Novelties

500 First Avenue   Stroudsburg, PA 18360

Mr. Richard Bache   February 2, 1982
Derwent Chemicals, Inc.
551 Northumberland Drive
Sarasota, Florida 64178

Dear Mr. Bache:

Please accept this desk pen and pencil set with our compliments. It's
a sample from one of our recent shipments to Chalmer's Manufacturing.
You'll notice that it bears the familiar Chalmer's logo.

These sets have proved a popular and effective sales device for many of
our customers throughout the country. When produced in quantities of
5,000 or more, they are quite inexpensive. They are far more impressive
than the usual gimmick giveaways, yet I think you'll be surprised at
their low cost.

We would like to show you more samples and tell you what Grayson
Novelties can offer your company. Just call 800-427-4567, and we'll
arrange an appointment.

Cordially,

T.J. Jackson
Sales Manager

letter. With this approach the name and address are individually typed on a preprinted letter—the same typewriter should have been used on the body text for printing as on the name/address fill-in. This will minimize the contrast and thus improve effectiveness.

The least expensive letter is the preprinted, impersonal "Dear Sir" letter. With this approach the entire letter is typed, then offset printed onto corporate letterhead stationery. A sample is shown in Figure 8-4.

Your Implementation

Some of the production of direct mail letters (printing, folding, inserting, sealing, stamping, sorting, and posting) may be done in-house to save cost. However, it can be much more efficiently handled by a mailing house and won't disrupt your clerical personnel. Because of the complexity of direct mail (it is truly an art form), I strongly recommend the use of a direct mail specialist to prepare the copy and to coordinate the entire program, from obtaining the list to counting the replies.

Consider direct mail as an evolving process. Don't judge its effectiveness on the first program only. Each of the three elements previously discussed—mailing list, letter, and implementation—can be improved over time. Sampling is a good way to test both the list and the copy. For example, a test mailing of 5,000 pieces that generates a 2 percent response indicates with 95 percent probability that on any identical mailing, the returns will be between 1.6 and 2.4 percent of the letters sent.

YOUR IMAGE—THE SOFTER SELL

Nearly all the larger companies and some small ones invest substantially in campaigns of advertising and public relations that don't directly sell products or services. Instead, these campaigns are designed to create a favorable image for the companies that sponsor them. Successful image-making may or may not help sell products, but its effect is positive: increased public trust and confidence. The universal message of all such campaigns, however

Figure 8-4.   Sample of a preprinted, impersonal gimmick letter. (Courtesy Boston Saw & Knife Corporation.)

BOSTON SAW & KNIFE CORPORATION
292 RESERVOIR ST. NEEDHAM, MA 02194 617-444-2051

SPECIAL ONE-TIME INTRODUCTORY OFFER: We'll sharpen any carbide saw — FREE
to prove a point or two . . .

. . . . like the fact that we're the carbide saw champ in this area . . . that our know-how and
service can help you cut the cost of cutting, and improve the quality too. But you'll never
know until you sample our services. That's why we're making this special offer:

WE'LL PICK UP, SHARPEN, AND DELIVER BACK ONE CARBIDE SAW,
ABSOLUTELY FREE . . . NO STRINGS ATTACHED.

Why try us? Aren't all saw sharpeners the same? Not by a long shot, and here's why:
Cutting performance depends on many factors; type of machine, condition of bearings and
guideways, material being cut, saw body type, saw fitting, operator skill, to mention a few.
We often check out our customers' cutting operations to see that everything matches up, to
make sure they're getting optimum performance. We take pride in our ability to make
suggestions to correct deficiencies in all these areas.

For example, a cabinet maker called us in because he was plagued by chipping and cracks
when cutting a double-sided laminate. We solved his problem by "borrowing" techniques
learned when dealing with a customer in an unrelated industry. We can do the same for
your cutting operations, no cost, no obligation on your part.

We invite your inquiry and urge you to take advantage of our free carbide saw resharpening.
Although we specialize in carbide, we handle all industrial grades and reputable blade
makers. Our only allegiance is to our customers, not the blade manufacturers.

To get your free carbide saw regrinding, just call me at 617-444-2051. The sooner you call
the sooner we can prove we're your best source in this area.

Yours truly,

Glenn P. Stewart

Glenn D. Stewart
General Manager

SALES and SERVICE: CARBIDE and H.S.S: MACHINE KNIVES · CIRC KNIVES varied they may be, comes down to "Here's a good company to do business with."

A good image in the marketplace naturally has value, even though that value may be difficult to measure. In supporting your sales program, it's wise to give some attention to steps that will enhance your company's reputation and thus help your salespeople do their job. There are three basic tools of image-enhancement, and they are readily available.

Articles in Trade and Business Publications

You may wonder why some companies get extensive write-ups in trade and business magazines and why your company doesn't. The fact is that most articles in most business publications are initiated, not by the editors, but by the companies seeking publicity. Recently I prepared an article for one of my clients, an industrial distributor who had added a new service he wished to promote. I hired a business writer from the local newspaper for $250, and photographs were taken by a photographer known by the client company. The writer had been recommended to me by the editor of the magazine in which we wished to place the article, so there was little doubt of its acceptance.

Normally articles like this one are written by advertising or public relations agencies. The point is that they are not difficult to put together or to place in most trade and business publications. (It's a different story, of course, with top publications like *Fortune, The Wall Street Journal,* or *Business Week.* They're not looking for handouts. Give them a try anyway, if you think your story is a good one. They just might be interested.)

In comparison to paid advertising, the article approach has three big advantages:

1. It will cost you far less money.
2. It is much more believable to the reader as editorial rather than advertising material.
3. It gives you greater leeway in explaining your company and your products in precisely your own terms.

And there's an extra bonus that should not be overlooked. Once an article is published, reprints can be ordered and used as mailer inserts or handouts.

Public Speaking

Speaking opportunities abound, and you should take advantage of them to further your company's interests. Don't be bashful about making known that you're available as a speaker to trade association meetings and local business organizations such as the Rotary, Kiwanis, and so on. Choose a subject related to your business but broad enough to interest your particular audience. "A Safari through the Regulatory Jungle," for instance, or "How We Used Marketing Techniques to Make Multitech-100 a Household Word," would appeal to a wide range of business people.

Don't be put off by your inexperience as a public speaker. Naturalness and sincerity count more than rhetorical eloquence. The main thing is to plan your speech so that it adds up to a meaningful message that's easily understood. Here are three tips:

1. *Prepare your speech well in advance of delivery.* Memorize its content—not every word, just the ideas in logical sequence. Practice in private, so that when you stand at the podium you can concentrate on your delivery and the audience, not on reading your notes.

2. *Outline the key points on a handout sheet.* Don't forget to include your name and company! Leave enough space between topic headings for notes. Pass the outline to your audience before the talk. They may want to jot down comments. If your talk goes over exceptionally well, you may want to flesh in the details of the outline on paper as a possible magazine article or a brochure to send to customers and business associates.

3. *Support your speech with visual aids.* This helps to maintain audience interest, strengthen your points, and encourage retention of the material.

Space Advertising

Except for displays in the Yellow Pages and business directories, space advertising should be designed to enhance your company's image (at least for the industrial sector of business). Space advertising works best for consumer products. Here, of course, television represents the prime medium. But with a basic nation-wide TV campaign costing hundreds of thousands of dollars, few firms can afford it.

It's best to support your selling program with less ambitious measures, such as direct mail, which I recommend as your prime media for developing sales leads. Smaller companies with consumer products and services should also use newspaper ads and radio spots in lieu of television.

Brochures

Brochures can be effective sales tools. Your salespeople can leave them behind after a first call, for example. A good brochure can highlight a product or service quickly and succinctly. It can tell the prospect enough to raise his or her level of interest so that the job of selling is relatively easy.

An invaluable aid to salespeople who work for distributors is the line card, which lists the products carried and manufacturers represented. Like brochures, line cards should be clear, readable, and straightforward. See Figure 8-5 for an example of the front and back of a well-designed line card.

Idea #69:   Design your brochures from the user's point of view. Take into account what he or she needs to know, and choose a logical sequence of presentation.

When you are ready to prepare your brochure or line card, keep in mind the following elements.

Size
How will the brochure be sent and delivered? If you plan to mail it, then it's most economical to have the brochure designed to fit into a #10 envelope. If the brochure is to be placed in the back pocket of a proposal folder, it should be 8 in. by $10^{1}/_{2}$ in.

Figure 8-5(a). Sample line card—front. (Courtesy Washburn-Garfield Company.)

WASHBURN-GARFIELD

100 Prescott Street
Worcester, MA 01605

CALL — EMILE ST. PIERRE · JOE RICHARD · STEVE DALTON · PAT MORRIS · JEFF RAWSON

STEEL PIPE
- **SEAMLESS**
  - ASTM A53: 2" thru 24"
  - ASTM A106: ⅛" thru 24"
- **ELECTRIC RESISTANCE WELD**
  - ASTM A53: 5" thru 24"
- **CONTINUOUS BUTT WELD**
  - ASTM A120: ⅛" thru 4"

OTHER PIPE AND TUBING
- BRASS · COPPER TUBING · PVC/CPVC
- FIBER GLASS · STAINLESS STEEL

FITTINGS
- **BRASS**
- **COPPER**
- **CAST IRON AND MALLEABLE**
- **FIBER GLASS**
- **FORGED STEEL**
- **FORGED STEEL FLANGES**
- **PVC · CPVC · POLYPRO**
- **STAINLESS STEEL**
- **WELDING**

MANUAL AND AUTOMATED VALVES

- **BALL VALVES**
  - APOLLO · LANCE
  - JENKINS · POWELL
  - WORCESTER
- **CHECK VALVES**
  - CENTERLINE · JENKINS
  - POWELL
- **PLUG VALVES**
  - POWELL

- **GATE & GLOBE VALVES**
  - JENKINS · STOCKMAN
  - POWELL · VOGT
- **NEEDLE VALVES**
  - JENKINS
  - POWELL
  - R-P & C
- **SOLENOID VALVES**
  - ASCO

- **BUTTERFLY VALVES**
  - BAY STATE CONTROLS
  - JENKINS
  - NORRISEAL
  - POSI-SEAL
- **SAFETY VALVES**
  - CONSOLIDATED
  - SWENDEMAN
  - WATTS

ENERGY-SAVING PRODUCTS

GAUGES & THERMOMETERS
- ASHCROFT

TEMPERATURE REGULATORS
- POWERS
- SARCO
- SPENCE

PRESSURE REGULATORS
- ASHCROFT
- MASONELIAN
- SARCO
- WATTS

TRAPS & STRAINERS
- ARMSTRONG
- BARNES & JONES
- HOFFMAN
- SARCO

PIPE INSULATION
JOHNS—MANVILLE

OTHER PRODUCTS
- AIR GUNS
- FILTERS/ REGULATORS/ LUBRICATORS
- PACKING
- PIPE TOOLS
- SPRINKLER HEADS
- SUMP PUMPS
- TEFLON TAPE

Telephones: Local, 617-753-7225 Toll Free, MA 800-382-6982 NH, VT, CT, RI, 800-225-7368

Figure 8-5(b). Sample line card—back. (Courtesy Washburn-Garfield Company.)

WASHBURN- GARFIELD
Founded in 1880

stocks and recommends these quality products from internationally known manufacturers. . .

AEROQUIP CORP.
Grooved Fittings
ALLOY STAINLESS (ASP)
Stainless Fittings
ARMSTRONG MACHINE
Steam Traps & Strainers
AUTOMATIC SWITCH CO.
Solenoid Valves
BARNES & JONES INC.
Steam Traps
BAY STATE CONTROLS
Disc-O-Seal Valves
BETHLEHEM STEEL
Steel Pipe
BONNEY FORGE
Weldolets & Threadolets
CELANESE PIPING
PVC Pipe, Valves & Fittings
CENTER LINE INC.
Butterfly Valves
CONBRACO INDUSTRIES
Apollo Ball Valves
Safety Valves
Water & Gauge Cocks
DOVER CORP./NORRIS DIV.
Butterfly Valves
DRESSER INDUSTRIES
Ashcroft Gauges
Ashcroft Thermometers
Consolidated Safety Valves
DUFF NORTON
Air Fittings
Air Filters, Regulators.
& Lubricators
DURABLA MFG. CO.
Check Valves
Sheet Packing
Gaskets
FACET ENTERPRISES
Air Filters
STANLEY G. FLAGG
Malleable Fittings
Cast Iron Fittings
Brass Fittings
Threadless Bronze Fittings
G & B FLANGE
Carbon & Alloy Flanges
GLOVER MACHINE
Cast Steel Flanges & Fittings
GREENE, TWEED & CO.
Palmetto Packing

ITT GRINNELL
Malleable Fittings
Cast Iron Fittings
Unit Heaters
HARVEL PLASTICS
PVC Pipe & Fittings
HAYWARD MFG CO.
PVC Valves & Strainer
Industrial Strainers
ITT HOFFMAN
Steam Specialties
HONEYWELL BRAUKMANN
Radiator Valves
Float Valves
IDEAL CORP.
Hose Clamps
IDEAL FORGING CORP.
Stainless Flanges
JENKINS BROTHERS
Bronze & Iron Valves
Cast Steel Valves
Stainless Steel Valves
Ball Valves
Butterfly Valves
JOHNS — MANVILLE
Pipe Insulation
JONES & LAUGHLIN
Steel Pipe
LASCO INDUSTRIES
PVC Fittings
A. Y. McDONALD MFG CO.
Gas Cocks
McDONNELL & MILLER
Controls
MCC POWERS
Steam, Water Regulators
MAIN MFG. PRODUCTS
Hydraulic Flanges
MASONEILAN
Regulators
NALGE CO. DIV.
Plastic Tanks
PENN. MACHINE WORKS
Forged Carbon, Alloy
and Stainless Fittings
PERMACEL
Teflon Tape

PHOENIX FORGING CO.
Tank Flanges
Weldolets & Threadolets
PLASTO-O-MATIC VALVES
PVC Solenoid Valves
PVC Regulators
POSI-SEAL
Butterfly Valves
THE WM. POWELL CO.
Bronze & Iron Valves
Cast Steel Valves
Plug Valves
Stainless Steel Valves
Ball Valves
R. P. & C. VALVE INC.
Bar Stock Valves
RECTORSEAL CORP.
Pipe Joint Compounds
REED MFG. CO.
Tools
REVERE COPPER
Copper Tubing
Copper & Brass Pipe
RIDGID TOOL CO.
Tools
SARCO CO. INC.
Steam Traps & Strainers
A. O. SMITH — INLAND
Fiberglass Pipe & Fittings
SPEAKMAN CO.
Safety Equipment
SPENCE ENGINEERING
Regulators
STOCKHAM VALVE & FITTINGS
Malleable Fittings
Cast Iron Fittings
Bronze & Iron Valves
TUBE TURNS
Welding Fittings
TUBE FORGINGS OF AMERICA
Welding Fittings
UNITED STATES STEEL
Steel Pipe
HENRY VOGT MACHINE CO.
Forged Steel Valves & Fittings
WATERMAN MACHINE
Carbon & Alloy Flanges
WORCESTER CONTROLS
Ball Valves
Control Valves
Actuators

WASHBURN-GARFIELD COMPANY · WORCESTER, MA 01605

Telephones: Local, 617-753-7225 Toll Free, MA 800-382-6982   NH, VT, CT, RI, 800-225-7368

In any event, it should fit in the salesperson's briefcase and the customer's file cabinet.

How many pages should it be? I recommend one sheet, two sides as a minimum; an 11 in. by 17 in. sheet folded in the middle to produce a four-page brochure as a maximum.

Text

The content should cover what the company does, how it does it (of minimum importance), what the company can do for the prospect (of maximum importance), and the company's background. Use as few words as possible. Key words should be underlined or italicized for emphasis. Most readers will skim the text, so be satisfied with making just a few important sales points.

Graphic Design

Graphics should be subordinate to the written word. Use a maximum of two colors, printed on colored stock. One or two illustrations (photographs or sketches) will enhance the brochure's message.

Put your company's logo, name, and address on the cover, together with a sketch or photo of your corporate facilities or another aspect of your business that will command attention. Set the text in a clear, readable typeface.

Cost

A two-color four-page brochure printed on a glossy stock with a press run of 5,000 currently costs about $2,000. Remember that the brochure alone will probably not sell your product or service. Its function is to convey information in a form that will supplement the spoken word. It will also create an image of your firm. With this in mind, you may wish to avoid the extremes of shabbiness on the one hand or ostentation on the other.

Proposals

Idea #70:   The proposal is one of the most underutilized selling items in the marketing bag of tricks.

Most industrial managers think of a proposal as a price quotation and leave it at that, or they place a quotation and product spec sheets inside a jacket folder and submit it as a proposal. These managers miss a golden opportunity to make their proposal a selling tool that emphasizes cost justification and company capabilities. As mentioned in Chapter 4, a good proposal accomplishes the following objectives:

- Delivering the proposal provides you with an excuse for revisiting the prospect and again asking for the order.
- It summarizes the reasons for buying your product through the written medium, which is more believable than verbal communication.
- It allows you to once again stress the features of your product and to rebutt the objections of the prospect.

Consider charging for the proposal if it is a complex one. This strategy weeds out the firms that are not really interested in your proposition and enhances the value of the proposal to the ones who do receive it. And be sure to include a carefully prepared sales pitch in every proposal. You can have an insert printed up and ready to attach to each proposal. A sample of such a preprinted "boiler-plate" part of a proposal is shown in Figure 8-6.

Give-aways

Idea #71: If you deal with a purchasing agent on an ongoing basis, give him or her the most valuable gift that you can, short of having the gift considered a bribe.

Purchasing agents generally have two traits in common: (1) they are human, and (2) they are underpaid. In the Boston area a favorite gift of value consists of four box seats from the vendor's season ticket plan for one Red Sox baseball game. (Most purchasing agents can't afford to buy tickets for the excellent viewing locations available to season ticket holders.) One of my favorite

Figure 8-6. Sample of "sales pitch" portion of proposal. (Courtesy Accudata.)

accudata
Who & What is it?

Accudata, Inc. is a data processing service company with offices in Avon, Massachusetts, and Pawtucket, Rhode Island. Accudata assists neighboring firms by:

1. Developing information systems to conduct their business more efficiently.
2. Providing a full range of data processing tools (including Digital Equipment Corporation computers) to make these systems operational.

Accudata is a financially sound company that has grown steadily since it was founded in 1971. Yearly sales now approximate $1,500,000. Our growth has been a function of excellent customer acceptance of our products and services.

This acceptance, in turn, is due to the dedication of our people - - now more than 30 in number.

Why choose Accudata?

Simply stated, why is it to your advantage to transact your business with us at Accudata? We are unique for four reasons:

1. <u>WE CARE</u>
    This may sound trite, but we <u>really do care</u> about each and every client. You can confirm our attitude of concern by contacting our clients and by looking at our negligible employee turnover rate, which is the lowest of any New England data processing service firm of our size.

The reason for our low turnover rate is employee pride. Our pride in Accudata can benefit you in two ways:

a. <u>Confidence</u>. You can be sure that the Accudata professionals assigned to you will work to the utmost of their abilities in order to meet your data processing needs quickly and accurately.

b. <u>Security</u>. You can be sure that these individuals will continue to work for Accudata and will be available to you for many years to come. Ask any of our customers.

2. <u>WE OFFER A FULL LINE OF SERVICES</u>
    Have you ever felt that you were being pressured into buying a particular product because it was the only one in stock? This cannot happen at Accudata. We offer every type of data processing service that you could ever need. Our objective thus is to match the right service with your need at this particular point in your corporate growth.

    For small to large user, our services include:

    -   <u>Service Bureau Processing</u>. Send us your payroll, inventory data, or other documents. We will process them at our datacenter and return the appropriate material to you.
        <u>Business Time Sharing</u>. In your office, we can install a terminal that is attached to our datacenter computer. On

your terminal, you can process your information on a shared-
time basis, without having the data leave your premises.
- In-house Computer. We can design, install, and implement any
  sized business computer (micro-, mini-, super-mini, or main
  frame) into your facility.
- Computer Consulting Services. If you already have your own
  computer, we can help increase its profitability by designing
  and implementing new systems and/or by loaning you a skilled
  programmer for peak load periods.
3. WE HAVE EXPERIENCE
   Because our programmers average more than three years each in
   our employ, they know the company and its procedures. They all
   have extensive knowledge of computers and computer languages,
   too. Most important, they are experienced in working on applications like yours. Background information on our executives
   is included in the last section of this proposal.
4. WE ARE SEPARATE FROM THE HARDWARE MANUFACTURER
   As a service firm, Accudata is separate from and smaller than
   our hardware supplier. Therefore, we seek an ongoing relationship with our clients, not merely a hardware sale. The well-
   being of each client is and must continue to be uppermost in
   our minds if we are to grow and enhance our reputation. Some

31 Memorial Drive/Avon, Mass. 02322 Tel. 617-584-6500
10 Summer Street/Pawtucket, R.I. 02860 Tel. 401-728-1470

firms are wary of having separate companies provide the hardware
and software services. In the case of Accudata, this concern
should be minimal. We take full responsibility for the <u>entire</u>
installation. In addition, we will remain your prime contact for
any problems that may occur in the future life of your computer.
Because we have enjoyed an extremely close working relationship
with Digital Equipment Corporation during the last four years, you
will have quick access to any additional support that you may
require.

We are as sound and financially healthy as any similar data processing service firm in New England. To verify this statement,
please feel free to check with Dun and Bradstreet; our bank,
Plymouth Home National Bank, Brockton, Massachusetts; or our
accounting firm, Laventhol and Horwath, Boston, Massachusetts.

accudata

Jeffrey Vendetti

Founder and president of Accudata, Jeffrey Vendetti has an extensive technical and applications background in all aspects of computer services.

Work Experience (most recent first)

Accudata, Inc.

- President. Founded the firm in 1971. Directed its expansion from an initial staff of six to its current size. Has spoken at various industry seminars on the use and selection of computer and communications systems. Has implemented a variety of systems for manufacturers, distributors, publishers, government, transportation, banking and others.

IBM CORPORATION, Waltham, Massachusetts

- Systems Engineer. Designed and installed systems for large-scale IBM users in the Boston area.

SAAMA, Kelly Air Force Base, Texas

- Systems Engineer. Involved with aerodynamic and structural projects for Air Force F-102 and F-106 aircraft. Administrered technical contracts in coordination with Hughes Aircraft Company and General Dynamics.

Education

CDP (Certified Data Processor), Data Processing Management Association

M.S., Mathematics, St. Mary's of Texas

B.S., Engineering Science, U.S. Air Force Academy

Technical

    Hardware: DEC, IBM, Honeywell, Burroughs

    Languages: COBOL, Assembler, FORTRAN, DIBOL, RPG, PL/I,
               BASIC

accudata

31 Memorial Drive/Avon, Mass. 02322 Tel. 617-584-6500
10 Summer Street/Pawtucket, R.I. 02860 Tel. 401-728-1470

William Meehan

A 1977 addition to Accudata's staff, Bill
Meehan manages the consulting operation.
He has a lengthy technical and managerial
background in the computer industry.

Work Experience (most recent first)

Accudata, Inc.

- Manager, Software Services.
  Manages the professionals who provide
  software services to Accudata customers.
  Personally directs projects to develop
  complex systems.

Keane Associates, Inc., Boston, Massachusetts

- Branch Manager, Westport, Connecticut.
  Supervised 18 employees in providing data
  processing services.

- Marketing Representative, Providence, Rhode Island.
  Conducted all marketing in the Providence area.

- Analyst, Providence, Rhode Island.
  Worked with specific clients in a variety of consulting functions.

Systems for Advanced Information, Inc., Rumford, Rhode Island

- Programmer/Analyst

- Programmer

Education

Graduate courses, University of Rhode Island

Introduction to Data Processing, Strayer College

A. B., English Literature, Providence College

Technical

Hardware: IBM, Burroughs, Honeywell

accudata

give-aways is the day-long deep-sea fishing charter, which costs the vendor approximately $400. If you invite eight purchasing agents at once, two can troll while the other six talk and drink beer. Your cost per agent is approximately $50, which is roughly equivalent to the cost of a dinner for two, and much more memorable!

Christmas gifts are the standard fare for many industries. Because they are so common, though, they have lost their distinctiveness and are often thought of as a requirement. For a novel and appreciated twist, try small birthday gifts.

CHAPTER 9

Growth by Internal Diversification

Many successful and even not-so-successful owners of small businesses are content to let their operation run at its own pace. They don't realize that the possibilities and advantages of planned accelerated growth offset the headaches and the dangers. Your commitment to growth should constitute a commitment to careful planning. At the outset, you should confront fundamental alternatives that need to be considered in the light of your particular circumstances.

First, you must decide whether it's best to develop new products and markets within your present organization or to acquire a company whose products and markets would give you instant diversification. One choice doesn't exclude the other, of course, and it's possible that you might decide to do both. But they should be looked at separately and in depth. In this chapter we focus on developing products and markets within your own organization, a process called internal diversification. In the next chapter, we discuss external diversification—growth by acquisition.

This chapter assesses the benefits and risks of diversifying through the four combinations of products and markets available to growth-minded businesses:

149

Present product/present market.
New product/present market.
Present product/new market.
New product/new market.

It's helpful to keep in mind that we're dealing with the horizontal integration of your company—that is, the development of a new product or a new market that parallels the products and markets you presently pursue. (Vertical integration consists in developing a product that contributes to the creation and/or sale of your present product, thus reducing costs or improving distribution. It's a sound concept, but it involves financial and organizational considerations outside the marketing purview of this book.)

Figure 9-1 presents a method of ranking the risks of your

Figure 9-1. Chance-of-success quadrants. (Source: A. T. Kearney, "Analyzing New Product Risk," *Marketing for Sales Executives*, January 1974, pp. 1–2. Reprinted by permission.)

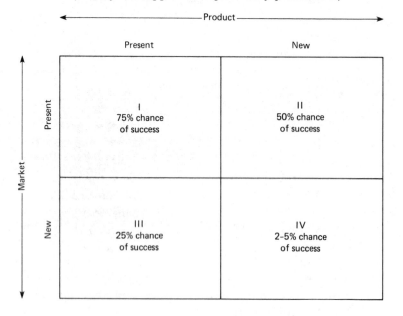

growth options. Based on a client project, it was designed by A. T. Kearney, Inc., a firm of international business consultants. The two-axis grid depicts the marketing options available and notes the approximate chance for success in each quadrant.

> **Idea #72:   The closer the new product is to what you are doing now and the markets into which you are now selling, the greater is the likelihood of success.**

Let's examine each option represented by the four quadrants of the grid in the light of its growth potential for your business.

PRESENT PRODUCT/PRESENT MARKET

As you can see in Figure 9-1, "present product/present market" has the highest success rating: Your chances of success are three out of four "because you are in your own ball park using your own ball," as the designers of the chart have said ("Analyzing New Product Risk," p. 1). Among corporate giants, IBM is probably the best example of success in this modified product approach. IBM constantly upgrades products, changes prices, alters promotion strategies, and offers new services in a continuing effort to make the most of its current lines and markets.

Krazy Glue, which you may remember from its spectacular television barrage in the mid-1970s, made millions of dollars in the consumer market by virtue of extraordinary promotion and mass distribution (its cyanoacrylate base was not new). It turned out that a major application was cosmetic—attaching artificial fingernails. Then, in 1979, there came a spinoff product, Instant Nail Glue for women—same product, same mass market outlets (drug, grocery, variety, discount, hardware, and department stores). All this goes to show that your present product in your present market can go far. In fact, in my experience and that of many marketers, it's the surest road to accelerated growth.

Idea #73: As your market expands and matures, actively seek out opportunities for variations and modifications of your product and how it is marketed.

How can you develop profitable product modifications? Here are four suggestions designed to get you thinking in the right direction:

1. Segregate your major user groups. Ask yourself (or a professional marketing researcher) the following questions: What specifically do these users want in my product? What features are applicable to their particular needs?
2. Consider adding a second line—either one with more bells and whistles for a higher price, or a stripped-down version for economy.
3. Review your line and your competitors' with your sales and product people to come up with improved models that will give your products a discernible edge.
4. Consider changes in other marketing elements:
   - Your pricing strategy.
   - Your methods of advertising and promotion.
   - Your approaches to sales and distribution.

NEW PRODUCT/PRESENT MARKET

The next-safest move is to take a new product to your present customers. According to our risk-evaluation chart, your chance of success is one in two (50 percent). That's better than the national rate on new product introductions.

In fact, there's less risk in introducing a new product to your present market than in introducing a current product to a new market. The reason is that in your current market you are well established. You know the buyers and how they operate. You know the competition, the pricing, and the service requirements. You are operating at relative strength when you bring a new product into your current market.* Indeed, it's estimated that new

* "Analyzing New Product Risk," p. 2.

product/present market offers *twice* the opportunity than the reverse.

The present market/new product option is commonly selected by major marketers everywhere. Procter & Gamble followed this route when it introduced Pringles Potato Chips. Within 18 months, P & G had 25 percent of the potato chip market! P & G could bring this off because it is long experienced in food store distribution.

Where do ideas for new products come from? You have two possibilities, passive and active idea solicitation.

Getting Ideas: Passive Solicitation

A good idea may come out of the blue. You don't know when or from where. That's why it's important to pay respectful attention to those inventors, friends, and employees who make suggestions for new products. Try to resist being cynical and thus unreceptive, even if you feel that most unsolicited ideas tend to be impractical. One good idea that you act on will make up for your patience with the ideas that didn't pan out.

Idea #74: Always respond positively to a new idea suggested by someone else—that is to say, consider its good features first before pointing out its weaknesses. A mind open to ideas is far more likely to find good ones than a closed mind is.

The history of business is strewn with poignant reminders of how experienced businessmen ignored or rejected good ideas. The predecessor of the Business Products Division of the Itek Corporation was one of a long list of firms offered the Haloid process. They turned it down. Well, Haloid became Xerox, and what a growth story that has been!

Getting Ideas: Active Solicitation

Of course, you don't have to wait passively for ideas. You can purposely generate them. One way is to appoint a "New Products

Planning Committee," whose function is to develop and evaluate new product concepts. It's customary to select representatives from the various operating departments—marketing, finance, engineering, and production—as members, so that you have a variety of perspectives and points of view in assessing new product possibilities. Be sure, though, that the members you choose have demonstrated creativity and imagination and are sales-minded enough to appreciate the value of a new product idea. Choose an enthusiastic, action-oriented leader who is committed to generating ideas and to moving decisively with the good ones. A strong, creative leader can overcome the natural inertia and bickering that sometimes afflicts such committees because of the varied background of members.

The New Products Planning Committee acts as a funnel for all the ideas for new products that come into your firm. That's its primary function, but effective committees go beyond mere screening to the active generation of ideas. You, the owner, should encourage idea generation either by being a member of the committee or by attending committee meetings often and letting members know that their job of fostering product ideas is of vital importance. Put a premium on bold, creative contributions, not on cautious rejection of all but the most uncontroversial ideas.

To generate new ideas the committee itself should broadcast its openness and receptivity. The fact that such a committee exists lets it be known throughout your organization and beyond that you welcome new ideas and will deal with them respectfully and courteously. When your committee generates a constant flow of new ideas, it becomes a forceful element in helping your company stay at the forefront of its marketplace. A flow of new product ideas energizes the atmosphere, keeps your people on their toes, and gives you a better-than-average chance of finding that one great idea that will make all the difference in profits and growth. Without this positive atmosphere, employees may be inclined to resist the work and risks that new products normally entail.

Remember, ideas are good only when you act on them. Prompt and reliable field evaluation must be part of the process.

Your New Products Planning Committee should nurture ideas

through a careful, step-by-step procedure. Follow these steps in order.

Step 1: Analyze your company's strengths, weaknesses, and direction.
Step 2: On the basis of your evaluation, develop criteria for new product selection.
Step 3: Assemble ideas. Some of the best sources of new product ideas are readily available. Check the following to make sure that you're touching all the bases:

Brainstorming.
Competition.
Consumer (focus groups).
Conventions.
Customers.
Customer service.
Foreign products.
Friends.
General Electric's "New Products."*
Government publications.
Goverment legislation.
Industry studies and surveys.

Inventors.
Outside agencies (advertising, patent attorney, design, and so on).
Peer personnel.
Research and development group.
Sales force and sales reps.
Senior management.
Suppliers.
Technical literature.
Trade associations.
Trade shows.

Step 4: Conduct a first screening. Screening an idea consists in systematically scrutinizing all important aspects in terms of your company's capabilities and the market potential. Every new product idea should be analyzed in light of information regarding:

* General Electric has a full-time staff that searches out under-utilized technology within its own organization and seeks buyers and licensees for that technology, which includes patents, know-how, technical publications, and product spin-offs. Contact GE's Corporate Research and Development Department, 120 Erie Boulevard, Schenectady, NY 12305, telephone (518) 385-2128.

- Size and growth of market segment.
- Market interest.
- Compatibility with current manufacturing techniques, tools, sales, and distribution setup.

Step 5: Ideas that survive the first screening should be subjected to a second. Once again, analyze:

- Size and growth rate of market, in detail.
- Size and type of competition and its approaches.
- Your proposed method of sales and distribution.
- Receptivity of buyers. Will they commit in advance?
- Cost-versus-return justification, including estimated sales and expense budget, two-year sales projection, and marketing expenses (hiring and training costs, advertising, trade shows, and so on).

Step 6: Commit to going ahead by production or acquisition.

Have your New Products Planning Committee meet at least once a month. Make sure that the committee leader commands respect not only of the committee members but of your entire organization. Monitor the market constantly while your new product is being developed. This is important because you need to know when a competitive product appears that might undermine the value of your product or necessitate a design modification. At the field testing stage, take time to eliminate any bugs in the product, even though this might delay its introduction or risk giving your competition time to develop a similar product.

Pricing Your New Product

Idea #75: Most manufacturers, particularly job shops, determine the price of their new products by calculating their overhead and adding a profit percentage. They exclude critical marketing factors, such as what price consumers will accept.

Pricing strategy can be overwhelming in its complexity. But it need not be. Here's my straightforward approach:

Idea #76:   Target a new product for the highest price level that a competitive market will accept. Then subtract costs, overhead, and a reasonable profit. If there is any money left over, launch the product. Otherwise don't.

Idea #76 focuses on two factors: market requirements and cost. Market strategy dictates whether to seek a limited volume at a high selling price and markup or a large volume at a low selling price and markup. For the small company, where personalized service can be used to support the product line, the former policy appears to lead to much greater profits. Owners of service firms seem reluctant to charge a higher price than their competition. This is often a mistake. Purchasers usually associate a higher price with better quality and service.

Competition and market conditions can change the accepted pricing level rapidly. In the 1970s housing prices doubled, yet in this same period digital watches went from $2,000 to $10. (The Swiss watch industry had predicted that parity in price between digital and standard watches would not be reached until 1985.)

PRESENT PRODUCT/NEW MARKET

In my definition, new markets encompass *new customer groups* (that is, sub-markets) and *similar customer groups* in new geographic areas (including overseas).

The majority of my client assignments involve taking existing products into new markets. The appeal of this approach is its apparent (but deceiving) minimal investment in effort and expense to take an existing (successful and debugged) product into a new market. But remember the risk-evaluation grid. "Present product/new market" is in the 25 percent quadrant—just a one-in-four chance of success.

Idea #77:   The underlying problem with taking an existing product into a new market is that the market usually dictates the product's features rather than the product creating its own acceptance.

A market is usually established with a well-defined method of doing a solid, knowledgeable, user-based business and with a stringent new product evaluation criteria. It is difficult for a newcomer to gain access and acceptance.

The Risks

Should you attempt such diversification, be on the lookout for the following problems:

- Your product may not have quite the proper balance of performance features (method of operation, speed, price, appearance, reliability, and size) demanded by the new market application.
- Competition may be entrenched. For instance, a client of mine wanted to sell its advertising specialty rulers to retail stationery stores, mass merchandise, and college bookstore markets. My client discovered that the competition had low prices, a well-earned reputation for quality of service, and a wide variety of related products. His product didn't have a chance against that kind of competition.
- Your firm and its products represent an unknown. Your company may be well established, but to new buyers and customers to whom you are unknown, that doesn't matter. Furthermore, should you wish to sell through manufacturers' reps or distributors you must start at the beginning in this new market. Those sellers, particularly the well-established reps with good contacts, are now carrying your competitors' lines.
- Lack of familiarity with a new field, plus ongoing demand for your current products, may give you good reason for not pursuing a promising new product idea.

The Rewards

On the other hand, taking your product into new markets successfully can offer a multitude of rewards.

- It can allow you to accelerate the growth of your firm. You will have two divisions or product groups rather than one.
- It will help you to reduce the risk of a market downturn or failure. If one market dries up, you still have the other.
- It provides the excitement and stimulation necessary to keep your management alive. It should also support more intense development of other new products in the markets now being served.

Markets to Consider

You have many options. Two that are often overlooked or ignored are the federal government and overseas markets.

Federal Government

Government agencies purchase anywhere from $100 billion to $240 billion in products and services each year, making Washington the world's biggest single market. Admittedly, there are difficulties in doing business with the government. Red tape, paperwork, bureaucracy, a plethora of regulations, special specifications, and slow decision making are some of the most common complaints. But if you look at these difficulties as simply hurdles to overcome, and then go out and get government sales, there are some distinct advantages:

- The federal government is a stable industry with minimum cyclical fluctuations.
- The possibility of obtaining repeat business is excellent.
- The federal government pays its bills, usually on time.
- All sales made to it are exempt from excise and sales tax.
- Often there is little or no competition.

The government buys an impressively broad range of products, from loose-leaf binders to rubber hoses, from office copiers to trucks. Lists of goods and services purchased can be obtained from these sources:

- *The GSA Supply Catalog* (published by the U.S. Government Printing Office, Washington, D.C. 20402). Costs $20 for an annual subscription and lists up to 20,000 commonly used products.
- *U.S. Government Purchasing and Sales Directory* (published by the Small Business Administration; available for $2.35 from the U.S. Government Printing Office). Gives complete information on the various federal purchasing offices and their product needs.
- *Commerce Business Daily* (published by the Commerce Department; available through Commerce Department field offices for $40 a year). Covers civilian agency procurement invitations for products or services costing $5,000 or more and for military items of over $10,000.

Sales and Marketing Management magazine, the source of these suggestions, also mentions Washington Researchers, a consulting firm located in Washington, D.C. This organization distributes *Washington Information Workbook*, which provides information on buying sources for various federal departments and agencies. Price: $35.00.

Selling to the Federal Government, written by Jack W. Robertson and published by McGraw-Hill, New York City ($16.50) is a very informative book about writing formal proposals.

Overseas Markets

When our family moved to Germany for two years in the late 1960s, I was amazed at how export-minded the European countries are. In Germany, there was a six-month wait for Mercedes Benzes; the automotive production was earmarked for export. The hi-fi speaker I wanted was unavailable because the firm's entire annual production was being shipped to the United States.

Yet small American companies are reluctant to attempt to sell overseas. This is unfortunate. Look at the larger corporations, which obtain anywhere from 10 to 50 percent (or even more) of their sales from the foreign market. In periods when the value of the dollar declines overseas, export sales become even more attractive to small companies as well as large.

To start selling overseas, contact your nearest U.S. Department of Commerce office. Someone there will gladly show you what the exports are, by country, in your product category, advise you about import duty rates, and tell you how to get into the exporting business itself. All for free.

One very helpful service that the Department of Commerce provides is access to foreign trade shows. These shows, held periodically in various foreign countries (usually one family of products is on display at a time), are funded largely by the U.S. government. The shows provide the participants with an opportunity to gauge overseas demand and to meet overseas sales reps in their home environment.

Once the market assessment has been complete, the next step for a small company with no export department or experience in overseas sales is to set up a sales network covering the desired foreign market areas. This can be done either through contacts made while exhibiting overseas at the U.S. Department of Commerce show or through a United States export consultant.

A local bank with a foreign department should then be identified. Bank personnel can help you with the financial side of the transaction, choosing between letters of credit, sight drafts and time drafts as payment instruments.

Finally, you will need to select a method of shipment. Large companies ship in full containers and firms requiring rapid delivery ship air freight, but most organizations use standard crated packages handled by freight forwarders. In addition to coordinating the shipping, a capable freight forwarder can provide advice on the entire shipping process and the paperwork involved therein. The rest is up to you!

NEW PRODUCT/NEW MARKET

The allure of greener grass often proves irresistible to the business person with an entrepreneurial or imaginative nature.

The introduction of a new product into a new market has provided me with my most exotic and educational research assignments. I'll never forget Bagarat, that nifty electronic rat trap I mentioned in Chapter 1. The world certainly did not beat a path to its maker's door, but I learned a fundamental lesson in marketing—the "better mousetrap fallacy."

From Cross-Newform, the plastic sign manufacturer who sought to introduce a tennis ball holder to be attached to a woman's tennis skirt, I learned how illusive quirks of human nature have an unanticipated effect on a market. It was a perfectly good idea that didn't sell, as we soon discovered, because women valued fashion over convenience and didn't like the way the holder altered their silhouette.

Other clients of mine have invested in seemingly good ideas that didn't pan out in the marketplace. A leading manufacturer of earplugs had hoped to take its noice-damping material to manufacturers of mining equipment; a successful paper company asked me to investigate the potential of a wind-activated, battery-powered bug spray for homeowners. Some of these products are far-fetched—and totally unrelated to the company's product or marketing expertise. But others have a tie-in. Cross-Newform's tennis ball holder required the same plastic materials and vacuum forming techniques used in making its signs.

Such product ideas are typically the brainstorm of one person, usually the owner of the company. The reason these ideas are pursued, whereas many other ideas or inventions are not, is that the owner has the funds and business skills needed for promotion and distribution. But the chances for success of a new product in a new market are small. As our grid chart demonstrates, the rate of success is approximately one in 20, or 5 percent.

Nevertheless, success can be realized! One of my clients, Seaboard Foundry, a custom caster of iron products, pulled it off with its first product—a new line of mushroom anchors. Seaboard is now the largest producer of mushroom anchors on the East Coast. Harry Sleicher, Seaboard's president and an avid sailor, thought of the idea while looking at the pleasure boats anchored in Narraganset Bay.

Success stories in the new product/new market category,

though, are not the stuff of which dreams are made. The risks are high and the chances for success slim. I recommend pursuing the new product/new market alternative through external diversification—by acquisition. With an acquisition you buy an ongoing, presumably profitable, and well-established entity. You are not starting from scratch. This fact changes the odds in your favor. Acquisitions as a path to accelerated growth should be seriously considered. We'll discuss them in detail in Chapter 10.

Growth by Acquisition

For many companies, the quickest and surest way to grow is by acquiring a going business that has the needed products and/or markets.

Clearly, finding the right company at the right price is the key. This is easier said than done. For one thing, it's nearly always a seller's market—there are more people looking to buy businesses than there are businesses for sale. In fact, potential buyers usually outnumber sellers by as much as 100 to one. So finding the right company entails much more than simply keeping your eye out for likely prospects, which is what most people do—with a notable lack of success. Most prospects have been picked over thoroughly by many other potential buyers. If the prospect wasn't for them, it may not be for you either.

Merger and acquisition consultants will conduct the search and assist in the negotiations. They can be helpful because they're professionals, and you may want to consider using their services. Keep in mind, though, that these services are expensive—most consultants charge a monthly retainer plus a commission on the sale. Another consideration is that employing a consultant tends to limit your range of prospects to those that the consultant selects. If you conduct the search yourself, you might look at more and better prospects.

164

Here's a phase-by-phase method that you can use to seek out suitable companies for acquisition.

PHASE ONE: PREPARATION

Draw Up a List of Specifications

Make the details of your list as precise as possible. Do you want a manufacturing, distribution, or service company? Include the type of product or service you seek, the location and any other pertinent preferences you may have. Also state the total amount of money that you have available to invest.

Your specifications sheet should also include background information about your own company, because you will distribute copies to prospective firms, bankers, accountants, and other specialists who might help you in your search. Figure 10-1 is a sample of the kind of specifications you will need.

Form a Team of Specialists

In order to pursue and close an acquisition you should have the help of specialists. It is a good idea to select them in advance. Your team members might include an accountant, a business associate, a lawyer, and a banker. The accountant and the lawyer will both be actively involved in the screening process. The business associate will provide a sounding board. If possible, the banker should be more of a friend than a supplier of business services, because you may not wish to confine yourself to one bank. Another bank or another form of funding may ultimately prove to be more advantageous, so you need to maintain flexibility in selecting the banking member of your team.

In dealing with these team members, keep in mind that they are advisers, and *only* advisers. You are the decision maker. I can think of two very successful business owners who purchased their businesses against the advice of their accountants. In both cases the accountants based their negative recommendation on the cur-

Figure 10-1.   Sample specifications sheet. (Courtesy Spenax Corporation.)

ACQUISITION SPECIFICATIONS

I.   SELECTION CRITERIA

    A. Product: Manufacturer of industrial (preferably consumable) metal products sold on an OEM basis. Examples are wire fasteners, tubular rivets, staples, industrial knives, and pumps.

    B. Location: New England

    C. Management: Some management continuity desirable

    D. Method of
        Acquisition: Cash (low seven-figure maximum)

II.   SPENAX'S BACKGROUND

Spenax Corporation is a privately owned manufacturer of fasteners and fastening tools sold primarily on an OEM basis to other manufacturers in such diverse markets as automotive, furniture, and agriculture.

Spenax Corporation employs 65 people and has annual sales of approximately $4,500,000. Headquarters and one manufacturing facility are located in Spencer, Massachusetts, with a second manufacturing facility located in Bad Axe, Michigan. Spenax is also involved with a joint venture overseas.

SPENAX CORPORATION · SPENCER, MASS. 01562 · TELEPHONE (617) 855-5332
MANUFACTURING FACILITIES: SPENCER, MASSACHUSETTS AND BAD AXE, MICHIGAN

rent financial status of the business. They could not envision the growth potential and its positive financial impact.

PHASE TWO: THE SEARCH

> **Idea #78:   Generate as many candidates for acquisition as possible. This is important because the more choices you have the better your chances of making a beneficial acquisition.**

There are three basic approaches to searching for acquisition prospects: the unsolicited rifle approach, the intermediary approach, and the broadcast approach. Used in combination, these approaches should generate 10 to 20 firms that are available for sale and that generally fit your criteria. Let's have a look at each approach.

Unsolicited Rifle Approach

One business in ten changes hands or closes every year. So if you contact an average of 100 businesses in a personal and professional manner, you will find that up to ten may be interested in talking to you as a buyer. Much depends, of course, on your professionalism in talking to such "cold" prospects. After you've clearly defined the kind of company you're looking for, check through the regional manufacturing and service directories in your area for likely prospects. This is laborious and time-consuming. You can save yourself the trouble by using Dun and Bradstreet's computer search, mentioned earlier in connection with the sales prospecting program. It costs about $1,200, but it's easy to use. Simply call a representative from D&B's Marketing Services and give the representative the profile information from your specifications sheet. In two to three weeks you will receive some 2,500 cards with the names of companies matching your specifications. Each card lists the firm's name, address, and telephone number.

In addition, you are given the president's name, a brief description of the major products and services, and the size of the firm in terms of sales and number of employees.

From this batch of cards, select the most attractive 100 to 200, which comprises a realistic population for your search. (You can select more, of course, but remember that it will take 10 to 15 minutes to call each company, and you will have to visit each company that responds positively.)

Next comes the mailing. This should include a transmittal letter and your specifications sheet. The transmittal letter should be personally addressed to the corporate president (in small and medium-size firms, that's usually the owner). The body of the letter can be automatically typed to save money. But be sure to state a particular time period during which you plan to call to determine his or her interest. Also, stamp the envelope and letter CONFIDENTIAL.

Figure 10-2 is sample letter of transmittal. The method I use, when helping a client search for potential acquisitions, is to mail out a batch of 100 letters early on a Sunday morning. The companies receive my letters on Tuesday, and then I call on Wednesday or Thursday. Friday is a follow-up day.

Intermediary Approach

The next group to contact are the intermediaries—accountants, bankers, and brokers, any of whom may know of firms for sale. Select the names of accounts from the American Institute of Certified Public Accountant's private directory entitled *Accounting Firms and Practitioners,* which can be obtained through your own accountant. Names of bankers can be obtained through the *Rand-McNally International Bankers Directory,* available at your local business library. Business brokers can be identified by looking for their advertisements in trade magazines and the Yellow Pages of large city telephone directories. Many will contact you when you advertise your search (discussed in next section), or you can write to people directly with a simple request similar to that in Figure 10-3.

Figure 10-2.   Sample letter of transmittal.

SALESMARK

THE MARR BUILDING ☐ 10 KEARNEY ROAD NEEDHAM HEIGHTS, MASSACHUSETTS 02194

(617) 449-3684

March 31, 1982

Mr. Ronald Arnesault
Butler Manufacturing Co.
80 Industrial Way
Hamden, Connecticut 06514

CONFIDENTIAL

Dear Mr. Arnesault:

Mr. Donald Hare, President of Spenax Corporation, headquartered
in Spencer, Massachusetts, has asked me to contact you to determine if your firm might be available as a merger or acquisition
candidate.

Mr. Hare is personally conducting this search with my assistance.
Specifications covering the type of candidate sought are attached,
accompanied by a brief description of the Spenax Corporation itself.

Please anticipate a call from me in the middle of the week to
determine your level of interest. As part of our conversation
I will explain why Mr. Hare wanted me to initiate this contact
and what he desires.

                    Sincerely,

                    Brooks Fenno
                    Brooks Fenno

Att.

SALES AND MARKETING SERVICES ☐ NEW PRODUCT ANALYSIS AND APPLICATIONS

Figure 10-3.   Sample request sent to an intermediary.

SALESMARK

THE MARR BUILDING ☐ 10 KEARNEY ROAD NEEDHAM HEIGHTS, MASSACHUSETTS 02194
(617) 449-3684

April 10, 1982

CONFIDENTIAL

Mr. John Mason
Mason, Rudkin & Co.
50 N. Main Street
Providence, Rhode Island 02903

Dear Mr. Mason:

Do you or any of your partners know of a manufacturing business
for sale that would match the attached specifications?

If so, please contact me at your earliest convenience. My
client, Spenax Corporation, is prepared to reimburse you for
your effort through a finders fee or otherwise.

Thank you.

Sincerely,

Brooks Fenno

Att.

SALES AND MARKETING SERVICES ☐ NEW PRODUCT ANALYSIS AND APPLICATIONS

Advertising Approach

The most productive medium for advertising when you're in the market to buy a business is *The Wall Street Journal*. A one-time ad, one column wide and one inch deep, costs about $250 and should produce 20 to 30 replies. Of these, perhaps five or six should prove promising enough to be worth further contact.

You might also try placing a similar ad in the "Business Opportunities" section of your nearest metropolitan newspaper. You will probably get a dozen or so responses, including some from business brokers and real estate agents. You will also get at least a few responses from principals interested in what you might have to offer. It's worth the try, if for no other reason than that the cost of such advertising is quite low.

PHASE THREE: THE SCREENING

When you have assembled a group of prospects with whom you have had a preliminary discussion over the telephone and who have expressed interest in discussing your proposal further, it's time to take a closer look by visiting each firm in person.

The First Visit

As you plan your visits, remember that you can compare the firms to one another more accurately by visiting them at close intervals. Don't plan to see more than two in any given day, however. Allow two hours for each visit. It often helps to bring one of your associates with you to compare notes and exchange ideas and opinions about what you hear and see.

Be prepared to submit your company's balance sheet and a bank reference to the potential sellers. Often they will ask for these before agreeing to meet you.

In any event, remember that your prime objective in the first meeting is to assess the "chemistry" between your company and the candidate for acquisition. Try not to be negatively influenced by the physical appearance of the firm if it happens to be in disrepair. Do be influenced by your evaluation of the following factors:

- *Product fit.* How well do you and your company relate to the products or services sold? How compatible are these products and services to your own background and that of your present company?
- *Proximity.* How far is this new business from your present office and plant? Can you drive to it in less than an hour?
- *Reason for selling.* Why does the owner want to sell? Is he under any particular time pressure to do so?
- *Selling price.* Does the owner have a particular price in mind? Is it rationally determined? (This is not the time to negotiate a selling price, but rather to determine whether the two of you are in the same financial ballpark.)

The Second Visit

On the basis of your initial visit, you will probably be able to reduce your list from 20 to five or six firms of particular interest and another half dozen of moderate interest. Allot at least a half day per firm for each second visit, including lunch with the owner. The purpose of the second visit is twofold: (1) to take a much closer look at the business (armed with all the questions you've thought of since the first visit) and (2) to examine the current financial statements. At this point the owner should not feel the need to be represented by an accountant or a lawyer.

Some of the non-financial considerations to be looked into on your second visit are:

- Does the company have a proprietary product, process, or service? (A meaningful patent position is extremely helpful.) If it is a wholesaler, how important and secure are the product lines it distributes?
- Is it a small company in a big market or the other way around? (A large company in a small market may have

limited growth potential.) What market share does it have? Is that share growing? Who are the major competitors?

- Is the customer base balanced, with no single customer accounting for more than 15 to 20 percent of the firm's gross volume? (An unbalanced customer base introduces an element of risk. The current owner may have a personal relationship with key personnel in these firms which could end when the owner departs.)
- Has the company been in business at least five years? What have been the sales trends during this period? If they've been static or downward, why?
- Is this business professionally managed? How old and how competent are the supervisory personnel? How long have these people been employed by the firm? How long have the salespeople or sales reps worked for the company?
- Are there any marketing or legal problems that are pressuring the owner into selling at this time?

On your second visit, you should also find out the answers to the following financial questions:

- Do up-to-date and complete financial records exist for the past five years?
- Does the cost of goods sold represent more than 50 percent of sales? (If so, that leaves little room for reducing expense overhead as a way of increasing profits.)
- Is the debt load excessive? What are the terms of debt repayment and with whom?
- Is the company profitable? How much potential profit is consumed by fringe benefits for high-ranking officers?
- Does the owner want to sell the company, the land, and the building in one package? (That's usually a better buy for the acquirer.)
- How modern are the company's financial controls? How does the firm determine its product costs? Does it use data processing for providing immediate operating information?
- Are the financial statements, particularly the inventory, certified by the seller's accounting firm? (If so, your ac-

countant will not have to become involved as early in the acquisition sequence as might otherwise be the case.*)

Sizing Up a Prospect

Once the second visit has been completed, and you and the would-be seller are still interested in each other, then—and *only* then—do you have a true prospect. Actually, at this point, it's best to have more than one prospect—three or four would be perfect, and even then you probably have less than a 50 percent chance of making a deal.

The next step is to find the skeletons in the closet. Every company has them—weaknesses that may not even be fully known to the would-be seller. And a seller who is aware of them certainly won't point them out. You, as the potential buyer, must try to identify the most important problems *before* you purchase the company, or you can be sure they'll emerge, along with the smaller problems, shortly after you've completed the acquisition!

Now let's look at the basic areas you need to explore in your meetings with the seller before you make a final commitment to buy.

Financial Picture

You should obtain the current balance sheet and income statements for at least the last three years, preferably for the last five years. These documents should have been prepared and certified by an independent auditing firm. You should also obtain copies of the corporate tax returns filed during these years.

You will also need an up-to-date statement of inventory valuation. Be careful as to who prepares the statement and how it is done. Is the inventory valued by the LIFO (last in, first out) or FIFO (first in, first out) method? How marketable are some of the items in the back room? Are they possibly just junk?

Don't forget to order a Dun & Bradstreet credit report on the firm. While you may not learn much from it, if the firm is privately held, every piece of information helps.

* Questions for second visit drawn from Morton Golper, "So You Want to Sell Out," *The New Englander*, November 1973, p. 25.

Physical Assets

Carefully examine all physical assets. Is the machinery operable? Is it still part of the production process? To what degree is it automated? If you are acquiring the building, it is advisable to have an independent engineer check it out, noting particularly the condition of the roof and the heating/cooling system. Also look for signs of flood damage.

Market Analysis

It is very important that you gain a valid picture of the marketplace in which your prospect operates. It is this marketplace and the relationship of your prospect to it that will, in large measure, determine how much growth you can expect from the acquisition. To gain such a picture you should explore the following:

- Is the market for the product or service growing or declining? What methods of advertising and promotion are being used?
- Who are the end users of the product or service? Who influences buying decisions? What are their titles? How loyal are they to their current suppliers?
- How well accepted is the firm in the marketplace? What is its reputation? How does it rate against its competition in price, quality of goods, sales coverage, and speed of delivery?
- What are the current sales forecasts? Check *Predicasts* (probably available in your local business library). *Predicasts* provides short- and long-range sales forecast statistics for individual products by SIC numbers. Accompanying each forecast is the date and page reference of the document (magazine article, government report, special study or whatever) from which the statistics were extracted.

Armed with this information, you should visit *at least* two purchasers (preferably more) of the company's product or service (secure the names from the Yellow Pages). When doing so, do not mention the name of your acquisition prospect. Simply say that you are doing an investigation of the industry. Ask for information about the industry, about your prospect, and about its competitors.

Employees

While your thoughts may be focused on the prospect's tangible products or services and physical assets, do not overlook the workforce which you would inherit. Become familiar with the background of each supervisor (get copies of their employment applications or resumes from the owner). Next, try to ascertain the level of morale of the production and shipping department personnel. If they are not unionized, have they ever had an authorized union vote? If so, when and why?

Finally, call a local detective agency (select from the Yellow Pages, if you don't know of one yourself) and ask for a background report on the owner. Such a report will cost but a few hundred dollars and should give you confidence that you are dealing with a person with no glaring personal problems (such as alcohol or drug abuse) and no criminal record.

PHASE FOUR:
FINDING OUT WHAT THE BUSINESS IS WORTH

Before entering into negotiations, you will want to determine as precisely as possible the value of the business you may buy. To do this, you will need the company's current balance sheets and its profit-and-loss statements for at least the past five years. (See Figures 10-4 and 10-5 for samples.)

Figure 10-4 is the actual balance sheet of a distribution company. Note that it indicates the net worth, or "book value," to be $2,542,173.36. Always remember, in determining net worth, that assets must be updated to reflect current, or fair, values in today's marketplace. The three categories that may need updating are machinery and equipment, inventory, and real estate.

Because this sample is the balance sheet of a distributor, machinery and equipment are not included. To update the company's inventory, a prospective buyer would simply count units and then compute costs by the LIFO (last in, first out) method. Obsolete or

Figure 10-4. Sample balance sheet. (Courtesy Bowers, Mayer & Company, Inc.)

BALANCE SHEET

December 31, 1981

ASSETS

Current Assets		
Cash in banks and on hand	$ 59,668.56	
Accounts receivable—trade	971,828.31	
Inventory, at cost	2,605,401.07	
Prepaid expenses	9,660.80	
Total Current Assets		$3,646,558.74
Other Assets		
Cash value of life insurance		112,882.02
Fixed Assets		
Real estate, equipment, vehicles,		
and so on, at cost	$ 438,833.82	
Less accumulated depreciation	195,549.31	
Net Fixed Assets		243,284.51
Total Assets		$4,002,725.27

LIABILITIES, CAPITAL STOCK, AND SURPLUS

Liabilities		
Accounts payable—trade	$ 468,489.78	
Notes payable—banks	798,528.16	
Accrued expenses	24,282.04	
State business profits tax payable	25,294.20	
Federal income tax payable	126,914.58	
Total Current Liabilities		$1,443,508.76
Total Long-Term Debt		17,043.15
Total Liabilities		$1,460,551.91
Capital Stock and Surplus		
Capital stock, common—no par value		
Authorized—200 shares		
Issued and outstanding—104 shares	$ 45,700.00	
Earned surplus, balance Dec. 31, 1981	2,496,473.36	
Total Capital Stock and Surplus		2,542,173.36
Total Liabilities, Capital Stock, and Surplus		$4,002,725.27

Figure 10-5. Sample profit-and-loss (P&L) statement. (Courtesy Bowers, Mayer & Company, Inc.)

FINANCIAL DATA

A. General Statistics

Year	Profit (Before Taxes)	Return on Sales	Net Book Value	ROI (Before Taxes)
1977	$223,378	5.1	$1,221,506	19.1%
1978	439,480	7.7	1,461,190	30.0
1979	619,285	9.3	1,778,535	34.8
1980	570,387	7.5	2,073,103	27.5
1981	904,305	10.7	2,542,173	35.5
Average	551,367			29.4

Adjusted Book Value: $2,842,173 (including real estate value of $300,000)

B. Profits and Cash Generated

Year	Sales	Gross Profit	Net Income (Before Taxes and profit sharing)	Profit Sharing	State and Federal Taxes	Net Profit After Taxes
1977	$4,401,058	$1,130,079	$223,378	$ 8,000	$ 99,890	$115,488
1978	5,688,588	1,567,366	439,480	10,000	225,334	239,996
1979	6,683,050	1,832,961	619,285	12,000	289,618	301,617
1980	7,597,572	1,986,334	570,386	12,000	281,818	276,567
1981	8,420,195	2,334,952	904,305	12,090	422,208	470,006

slow-moving items can be written off. This company owns real estate, for which a current appraisal should be obtained. The net worth entry can be adjusted by adding or subtracting the difference between current value and book value from the fixed assets.

The P&L statement in Figure 10-5 depicts five years of financial data gathered from historical balance sheets and profit-and-loss statements. Part A shows profit before tax, the return of sales, the net book value, and the return on investment for each of the past five years. From this information we can compute the average return on investment. The statement shows the most recent net book value to be $2,542,173 and the adjusted book value to be $2,842,173. Part B records the sales, gross profit, net income before tax, amount paid to profit-sharing plans and taxes, and the net profit after taxes for the same five-year period.

Now let's see how we can use the balance sheets and P&L statements to determine values. There are *four* methods. They were prepared for this book by James W. Bowers of Bowers, Mayer & Company, Inc., a prominent Boston financial consultant and business broker.

Method 1—Adjusted Book Value Plus Goodwill

Let's assume that the seller of this company overlooks the fact that "goodwill" is rarely recognized as a value for distribution companies (because goodwill values usually accrue to manufacturers) and computes its value into the selling price.

What is goodwill? It is the value of a business's favorable reputation beyond the actual worth of what it sells. There are all sorts of formulas for computing goodwill. As a practical matter, however, *above-average* earnings are normally considered the best evidence of the existence of goodwill. The value placed on goodwill at the time of sale is often determined by capitalizing extra earnings. Before we can capitalize those earnings, though, we have to determine the normal return on investment in this particular industry. A good place to find this is in *Annual Statement Studies*, published by Robert Morris Associates, Credit Division, Philadelphia National Bank Building, Philadelphia, PA 19107.

The normal return on investment for the industry (18.2 percent in the case of our example) is then multiplied by the adjusted book value (from Figure 10-5) to yield the expected profit before taxes:

$$18.2\% \times \$2,842,173 = \$517,275$$

"Excess profits" are computed by subtracting the expected profits from the company's actual five-year average profits before taxes:

$$\$551,367 - \$517,275 = \$34,092$$

The seller then capitalizes goodwill by dividing the excess profits of $34,092 by 18.2 percent:

$$\$34,092 \div 18.2\% = \$1,873,186$$

$1,873,186 is the amount of cash required to get that return, at 18.2 percent, and is the seller's monetary assessment of the company's goodwill. This is added to the company's adjusted book value to yield the overall value of the company:

Adjusted book value	$2,842,173
Goodwill	1,873,186
Total	$4,715,359

Method 2—Discounted Future Earnings

Many sellers claim the value of their business to be the future earnings discounted to present value. To compute this, it is necessary to use pro forma figures for sales, cost of goods sold, and operating expenses by individual line item for five years into the future and to discount the net earnings by a percentage factor of risk.

In other words, we must determine the value of the future profits in today's dollars. The lower the percentage, the less the risk. A discount greater than 15 percent would be highly risky; a discount of 2 percent would suggest guaranteed profits.

Today's market carries all sorts of risks, known and unknown, so we will use a 12 percent discount. The computation, allowing a pro forma computation of sales and profits using historical growth of sales, cost of goods, and operating expenses to determine future profits (from Figure 10-5), is as shown in Table 5. Note that five-year future earnings were estimated most conservatively to be $4,521,000, for which, under this method of evaluation, one might be willing to pay $3,448,099.

Method 3—Adjusted Book Value Plus Discounted Earnings, Divided by 2

This method of valuation is the most conservative and covers the buyer's risk that earnings may falter for reasons beyond control. As the name indicates, the adjusted book value (from Figure 10-5) is added to discounted earnings (from Table 5):

$$\$2,842,173 + \$3,448,099 = \$6,290,272$$

This figure is then divided in half, giving the average of the two amounts:

$$\$6,290,272 \div 2 = \$3,145,136$$

Method 4—Return on Investment

This method requires the buyer to predetermine an acceptable return on investment. A 20 percent ROI is equivalent to five times

Table 5.   Discounted future earnings.

Year	Sales	Profit Before Taxes (Net Earnings)	12% Discount	Value
1982	$ 9,262,000	$ 740,000	.893	$ 660,820
1983	10,188,000	815,000	.797	649,555
1984	11,206,000	896,000	.712	896,000
1985	12,326,000	986,000	.636	627,096
1986	13,558,000	1,084,000	.567	614,628
Total		$4,521,000		$3,448,099

earnings; a 25 percent ROI is equivalent to four times earnings. In computing this value we'll use two different approaches: the historic approach and the potential average earnings approach.

The historic approach bases all calculations on the known average profit before taxes. In our example, the five-year average is $551,367. Thus, an acceptable ROI of 20 percent yields an historic value of:

$$\$551,367 \div 20\% = \$2,756,835$$

If the predetermined acceptable ROI is 25 percent, the historic value is:

$$\$551,367 \div 25\% = \$2,205,468$$

The potential average earnings approach bases its computations on the pro forma figure for future profits (before taxes), arrived at in Table 5. You'll recall that the five-year *total* was $4,521,000. The yearly average is then $904,200, and the calculations for a 20 percent and a 25 percent return are, respectively:

$$\$904,200 \div 20\% = \$4,521,000$$

$$\$904,200 \div 25\% = \$3,616,800$$

These examples show how you can use a balance sheet and a P&L statement to compute a wide range of values for the same company:

1. Net book value	$2,542,173
2. Adjusted book value	2,842,173
3. Adjusted book value plus goodwill	4,715,359
4. Discounted earnings	3,448,099
5. Adjusted book value plus discounted earnings, divided by 2	3,145,136
6. Historic value @ 20% ROI	2,756,835
7. Historic value @ 25% ROI	2,205,468

8. Potential earnings @ 20% ROI		4,521,000
9. Potential earnings @ 25% ROI		3,616,800
10. Average of above values		3,310,138

Given these figures, the seller will most likely ask $4,715,359 for the business. It's the highest figure, so he becomes an immediate convert to the "adjusted book value plus goodwill" method. You may, with equal aplomb, counter with an offer of five times the company's historic earnings: $2,756,835. Let the negotiations begin!

This is the critical stage. Bear in mind that negotiations are a human, give-and-take process. The four commonly used methods of evaluation should be thought of as guidelines, not laws cast in stone. Be flexible!

There is, however, one principle that, I think, should always be followed.

Idea #79: Pay only for past performance or present value of assets. Future success or failure is created by, and belongs to, the buyer. Don't pay for it!

PHASE FIVE: REGROUPING AND MAKING AN OFFER

You have decided that this is the company you want and, even more important, that the seller is willing to part with this firm and that you will be able to negotiate a mutually agreeable price.

Idea #80: Try to gauge the owner's willingness to sell. Sometimes an owner, especially one who is the founder, finds it extremely difficult to part with the company. Such an owner may seem willing at the outset but will balk at closing time.

Now come the final steps. With some luck you will want to make an offer, and the offer will be accepted. But first, review the prospect with your team. It is time to enlist the professional advice of your accountant, your lawyer, and your "friendly" banker. Keep in mind that in the final analysis you are the decision maker who must determine whether the business fits, to what extent you can benefit from its acquisition, and what you can contribute to its success. Also keep in mind that combined accounting and legal fees may run $5,000 to $20,000 and more, if the transaction is complex.

The Accountant

Ask your accountant to look closely at the earnings, assets, and liabilities in the records that you have obtained. Remember, these financial statements are prepared in the seller's interest! Then have the accountant draw up a projected cash-flow statement that will adequately cover both debt service and funding of growth. Guard against unrealistic optimism. It's better to be conservative at this point.

The Banker

Approach the bank with which you wish to do business, meet the banker with whom you would be working (possibly one and the same as your friendly banker). Determine whether this is the sort of firm you might be able to fund through that bank, considering your new worth, the type of business involved, and the type of assets that the firm can offer as security.

Then, with the aid of your accountant, develop a basic funding request and prepare an offer including price and conditions for the purchase. You can present this offer orally to the would-be seller as sort of a trial balloon by saying, "Mr. Seller, if you will accept $3,145,136 for your business under the following terms and conditions of sale [state conditions], then either my lawyer or yours can draw up a purchase and sale agreement. . . ."

PHASE SIX: MAKING A DEAL

The sequence of negotiations and the rules and regulations are only half the story. The other half is interpersonal, the part with all the glamour and excitement—getting you and the seller together on a basis that is advantageous to you.

Idea #81: If there is no pressure to close a deal, it will not be done.

Idea #82: If the seller has bad advice, you usually can't make an advantageous deal.

These two ideas are favorite sayings of Chet Krentzman, the renowned Boston deal-maker.

Also, keep in mind that with very small companies (those with sales of $2,000,000 or less), the price that the seller is willing to accept may be less influenced by logical valuation methods than by the seller's emotions. The negotiated price often reflects the dynamics of how much the seller wants to sell, how much the buyer wants to buy, and how many buyers are interested.

The Purchase-Sale Agreement

Assuming that the buyer and seller have agreed on the price and terms, then the purchase-sale agreement is prepared. Traditionally, the buyer's counsel draws up the agreement. But this agreement must reflect the wishes and idiosyncracies of the seller, and your lawyer should be given ample opportunity to become personally involved with the seller to become aware of particular personal concerns and wishes. Make certain that you read the small print before signing and that the people you are dealing with have the power to sign.

Terms that will void the agreement between the time that it is signed and the close should include:

- Inability of the buyer to raise the necessary purchase funds.
- Misrepresentation by the seller of continued customer purchasing plans.
- Lack of transferability of the lease, if the building and prop-

Figure 10-6.   Illustration of a leveraged buyout. (Source: Nick Galluccio, "Do You Sincerely Want to Be Rich?" *Forbes*, June 24, 1978, p. 38. Reprinted by permission.)

GOING WITH THE LEVERAGE

Among the many cases of "leveraged buyouts" in recent years, no company illustrates the balance-sheet risk in such deals better than Vapor Corp. Divested by Singer Co. in 1972, Vapor was purchased by its management in a $37-million transaction. At the time, its debt-to-equity ratio was 7.6-to-1, as shown by its balance sheet.

Long-Term Debt	$33.5 million
Stockholders' Equity	4.4 million
Total Capitalization	$37.9 million

In the five years since the buyout, management has repaid the bulk of the debt and reversed the balance-sheet ratio. Its debt-to-equity now stands at 0.35-to-1:

Long-Term Debt	$10.6 million
Stockholders' Equity	29.9 million
Total Capitalization	$40.5 million

Below, the company's debt principal repayment schedule since the buyout. Brunswick Corp., liking the looks of the company, last month signed an agreement to purchase Vapor Corp. for $90 million.

Repaying the debt (in millions of dollars):

	1973	1974	1975	1976	1977
Cash Flow	3.1	3.6	6.1	16.3*	7.9
Debt Repayment	1.1	1.4	2.6	15.0	1.6
Unrestricted Cash	2.0	2.2	3.5	1.3	6.3

*Includes $10 million raised in public offering.

---

erty are not being acquired and the buyer wishes to remain in the current location.

- Uncovering of past litigation, potential regulatory problems, or labor claims.

The purchase-sale agreement is then signed. Typically, the agreement will allow the buyer 30 to 90 days to raise the purchase funds and conduct the investigation as specified in the terms of the agreement.

A wise seller will continue to look for buyers at this point, recognizing that there is still a significant possibility that the deal will not be finalized. The buyer may ask the seller to take the company off the market. The buyer may offer the seller a non-refundable deposit of, say, $25,000 as a sign of good faith, as a method of obtaining the rights to visit key accounts, and as an incentive for removing the firm from the market.

The Closing

Ideally, the closing is a formality—but be careful. It can be booby trapped. Watch out for situations in which the seller has other than his accountant and lawyer present. The more people who get into the act the more potential problems in this final hour.

PHASE SEVEN: FUNDING YOUR ACQUISITION

The current trend in paying for an acquisition is to put up as little of your own money as possible and to borrow the rest against the assets of the business being acquired. This is called a "leveraged buyout." Generally, you let the normal operation of your newly acquired business pay off your loan in a period not to exceed five years. An example of how a leveraged buyout enters the books and how it is repaid is shown in Figure 10-6.

Post-Sale Relations

It is advisable, for several reasons, to carry the former owner on the payroll for a year or more:

- Paying the former owner as a consultant will provide you, the new owner, with a means of buying the company with pretax (expense) dollars.
- It keeps the former owner from starting a competitive firm or defecting to a competitor.
- It allows you to create, in the eyes of the firm's customers, a gradual and orderly shift in ownership.

Most merger and acquisition specialists do not recommend that you announce at once, to all your acquisition's customers, that you have acquired the company. To do so suddenly might give them the incentive to switch to another supplier who has been wooing them for years. Let your customers learn gradually. Any telephone calls for the former owner should be directed to and handled by him if he continues on your payroll for the period of his full-time employment.

Finally, you should meet regularly with the former owner to learn the technical and administrative idiosyncrasies of the business.

Funding Your Growth

Why is a chapter on finance included in a marketing book? Because it takes money to make money, that's why. You need cash in hand or credit to start a business, to maintain its normal growth, and to accelerate its growth through new products or acquisitions.

Where do you get this money? For most small businessmen the best way to raise capital is to borrow it. Borrowing wisely and well is an art in itself, and we shall discuss it in detail in this chapter, but first let's consider other alternatives.

EQUITY CAPITAL

Sources Outside the Company

Selling shares in your business constitutes a legitimate and attractive way of raising money for growth. There are many pitfalls, though. The main pitfall, of course, is that you, the owner, could be in danger of losing control. Each share you sell dilutes your ownership position to the extent that minority shareholders may at some point be able to band together and gain control.

But sometimes "going public" seems the best way—perhaps the only way—for a small business to raise the capital it needs.

189

Idea #83:   While friends often seem to be good prospects to buy into your company, you often jeopardize your friendship by involving them in your financial affairs. Even if the business grows and your friends prosper, the nature of your friendship will change.

Watch out for venture capital firms, too. Sometimes these outfits seem attractive because they offer financial and managerial advice as well as money. But always keep in mind that venture capital firms take a large portion of the ownership in exchange for their investment, and they are likely to push too aggressively for your firm's rapid growth—with a view to selling out or going public at a time that's profitable for them but may not be for you.

Another source of capital that often tempts small owners is a partnership in which two or more individuals invest equal funds for equal shares in the business. Here again I advise caution. Equal partnerships usually don't work out. If you're considering the partnership route, make certain the partners are not exactly equal in their voting rights.

Idea #84:   Remember that you will probably see more of your partner than you will of anyone else—even your spouse. Disagreements are inevitable, and when they arise, you need a single decision maker, preferably you.

Funds from Inside the Company

Before making commitments outside your company that will increase your obligations, dilute your ownership, and put you in debt, it's a good idea to see how much cash you can scare up through more efficient management of your own organization. Consider these often untapped, internal sources of growth money:

- Inventories are a frequently used source of idle funds. A typical small business will carry between 20 percent and 50 percent excess inventory in stock.

- Idle assets such as fixtures, equipment, materials, and so forth may be simply sitting around collecting dust. They could possibly be converted to cash. Excess space may be rented or subleased.
- Operating expenses can sometimes be reduced. As owner, consider taking less out of the business. Or, certain operations performed in traditional ways may be shifted to less expensive methods. Stop paying for services you can perform yourself. Exercising closer and tighter control over payroll, rent, publicity, and other regular monetary outlays can reduce costs.

There's a short-term, emergency approach to raising money that I increasingly encounter but cannot in all conscience recommend. This is to pressure customers for quick payment of receivables and to delay, by an extra 30 to 60 days, your payment of payables. This is certainly not a sound strategy for funding growth, but it can be used as a cushion in emergencies.

THE SOURCES OF BORROWED CAPITAL

Even with soaring interest rates, borrowing the money to fund your growth has much to recommend it. For small businesses, the best sources of loans are commercial banks, the Small Business Administration (SBA), and Small Business Investment Corporations (SBIC). There are other possible sources too, which should be considered.

Idea #85:   A business loan should be a business transaction, not a favor to the borrower by the loaner!

This is simply to emphasize what I've already said about the danger of involving friends or relatives in your money-raising efforts. No matter how pleasant and easy such deals look at their inception, be aware that they often turn sour—in human as well as financial terms. It's far less troublesome to deal with professionals when raising capital. For one thing, the professionals—that is, the standard loaning institutions—are familiar with the needs of small businesses. They can provide you with ongoing financial advice that can help you build your business. Let's have a look at them.

Commercial Banks

These are the major lending agencies used by small business owners for borrowed capital. Their methods of processing loan applications vary, and you should be aware of the differences. In some banks you may borrow money for business use from the consumer loan department. Other banks have special small business departments for this purpose. Others will delegate your request to a single officer for processing. Obviously, it makes little difference how your bank handles its formal procedures—as long as you're able to get the money to carry out your expansion plans!

Remember that semi-term loans of 30 to 90 days, for example, can often be renewed on a continuing basis under favorable circumstances. As your business grows and prospers, both the amount and duration of such loans may be increased.

Idea #86:   Remember the bank makes its money by loaning you money. The major concern to the banker is the risk involved in your ability to repay on time.

Commercial banks should be considered a source for debt rather than equity capital, but sometimes the two can overlap. Most short-term loans are for less than a year in duration, but many banks make long-term loans ranging from one to ten years with an average maturity of about five years. Loan types include:

Collateral loans (covers most long-term loans). Secured by assets with a value well in excess of the amount of the loan.

Character loans. Unsecured term loans that tend to be for shorter periods and smaller amounts than collateral loans. A person with proven managerial ability, an excellent reputation, and a sound business proposition may receive a character loan for several thousand dollars on a long-term, favorable interest basis at one bank, whereas another bank would require collateral from the same person.

Installment loans. Can range from $100 to more than $5,000. These loans usually require monthly repayments with the balance being due in a year or less.

Loans secured by accounts receivable on either a notification or non-notification basis. In the former case the bank notifies the borrower's accounts and attempts to collect receivables directly from them. In the latter case the borrower's customers may not learn that their accounts were assigned to the bank unless these customers fail to settle their accounts. In such a case the bank is likely to contact the delinquent account and assist in collecting the monies owed.

Loans secured by negotiable warehouse receipts or field warehouse stocks. Such loans are common for manufacturers and some dealers in heavy items such as furniture.

Equipment loans. May in some cases be obtained on more favorable terms from a bank rather than from the equipment manufacturer or supplier directly.

Mortgage loans. Made on the basis of chattel mortgages, personal or business property, or real estate mortgages that are owned either by the business or by the loan seeker apart from the business.

The banker will require a loan contract covering all the provisions that he or she feels are necessary to ensure repayment. Such a contract will cover the length of the loan and the repayment schedule; interest and other charges; provisions for default; requirements for the level of working capital; description of assets and terms under which they are pledged to secure the loan; restrictions on the payment of salaries and dividends during the duration of the loss; and miscellaneous other requirements.

In making a loan to the owner of a small business, the banker will take into account the moral character of the applicant, the managerial ability of the applicant, the nature of the loan (have loans of similar type been successful for the bank?) and the collateral offered to insure payment. The banker will need reliable facts to use as a basis for making a loan. For an ongoing business, the banker will want to analyze its balance sheet and income statement. For a new venture the banker will want a prospectus stating estimated sales, expenses, and profits.

Since collateral is so often required to secure bank loans, you should be familiar with what a banker considers to be good or bad collateral. Some of the items that *cannot* readily be converted into "quick cash" by a banker and thus do not provide collateral items include:

- Specialty machines, equipment, fixtures, or built-in construction not salable to others.
- Items carrying the name of the concern, such as stationery, signs, wrapping paper, or souvenirs.
- Merchandise likely to become outmoded because of changes in standards or styles.
- Unfinished products or assemblies for a particular buyer or market that has ceased to exist.

Some of the most common forms of collateral are:

- Accounts receivable.
- Inventory, valued at 50 percent of your listed worth.
- Machinery, valued at its auction worth ("hammer price").
- Real estate.

Small Business Administration

Under Section 207 of the Small Business Act of 1953, as amended, the Small Business Administration is empowered to make loans to small business concerns to finance plant construction, conversion, or expansion, including the acquisition of equipment, facilities, machinery, supplies, or materials; or to supply such concerns with working capital to be used in the manufacture of articles, equipment, supplies, or materials for war, defense, or essential civilian production or as may be necessary to insure a well-balanced national economy.

Under this Act the SBA is not empowered to make loans when the would-be borrower can borrow funds from conventional sources on reasonable terms. Furthermore, SBA loans cannot exceed $500,000 in any one case (often lower limits are imposed by the SBA to conserve funds) and cannot exceed 10 years for the purpose of construction or expansion, or for the purchase of machinery and equipment. Working capital loans are for five years; machinery and equipment loans for 10; and real estate loans for 20. The SBA also guarantees up to 90 percent or $500,000 of the loan (whichever is less). Interest on a direct loan is, as of 1981, 9.25 percent. Interest on a bank guaranteed regular term loan is the prime rate plus $2^1/_4$ percent for under 7 years or $2^3/_4$ percent for 7 or more years.

SBA loans do require collateral although, in practice, the SBA tends to be much more lenient than a commercial bank on what it will accept in this regard. The SBA generally will accept almost any tangible business or personal asset, whereas a bank will accept only liquid assets.

Small Business Investment Corporations

Another way in which the SBA assists in the financing of small business is through the licensing and regulation of small business investment companies (SBICs). This was made possible through the Small Business Investment Act of 1958, and was designed to provide small business with long-term debt funds and equity capital. In addition to granting long-term loans, an SBIC may provide financing for a small business by purchasing its capital stock or debt securities, or by purchasing debentures that are convertible into stock.

An SBIC is limited by law to a maximum investment in any single firm of 20 percent of the SBIC's combined capital and surplus. Thus if a business needs more money than one SBIC is permitted to provide, several may join in the financing.

Loans must have a maturity of not less than 5 years and not

more than 20 years. While debt securities cannot have a maturity of less than 5 years, there is no maximum maturity provision except as may be imposed on a policy of the individual SBIC.

Trade Financing

Trade financing is simply a method of buying materials, merchandise, or equipment on credit. Equipment manufacturers and dealers recognize that the average owner of a small business may not be able to pay cash for expensive installations and may have difficulty in obtaining bank loans for this purpose.

You can also take advantage of the standard credit plans offered by most major companies. Typically, these plans require a down payment of 20 to 30 percent of the purchase price, the balance to be paid in monthly installments over one to two years.

Some companies will simply offer credit on an extended basis to ease the financial pressure on a customer. This practice is prevalent in the retail field.

Miscellaneous Sources

Sometimes businesses or communities will financially help a new company relocate to a particular area. For example, a manufacturer of building materials might want a distributor located in a fast-growing city like Houston. Or a community that wishes to broaden its industrial base may offer liberal financial concessions in the form of tax rebates to new or relocating companies as an inducement to set up shop in a certain location.

People with property interests, such as developers or real estate agents, will often assist in securing initial financing of equipment and fixtures. And there are other sources of funds as well:

- Large distributors may finance small manufacturers to produce items for private label merchandising.
- Commercial credit companies may make loans on accounts receivable.

- Sales finance companies may specialize in buying a dealer's installment account paper at a discount.

Idea #87:   The best source of funds for acquiring a company is often the seller. Furthermore, the interest rate offered is usually several points below prime, as no banking or other institution need be involved.

Idea #88:   Don't limit the amount of funds you seek to borrow to a bare minimum. Allow enough of a cushion to cover all possible overlooked costs.

THE ART OF BORROWING

After you've selected the lending institution, you have to apply all your selling skills to get a loan. You want to make a persuasive case for your loan request, one that will assure the loaning agency of the security of its investment and of your integrity, professionalism, and good business judgment. There are three stages in the process, each of which should be given your full attention.

1. Preparation

Your loan application is your basic selling tool. It should be a document from which the lender not only learns the type of collateral security you're offering but also the "flavor" of the loan itself. The application should give the lender information about what kind of person you are. How capable are you in dealing with financial data? How articulate are you? How logical? What are your growth plans and projections? These are some of the questions in the lender's mind.

Obviously, the critical elements of your application to a professional lender are the type and amount of the security you offer.

Idea #89:   Your application is in competition with others. Make your application a selling tool by including all the "plusses" about yourself and your company that will influence the lender in your favor.

Here are the principal elements of a loan application:

Cover. Insert the loan application into an attractive binder.

Title page. Include the subject title (that is, loan application request), the name of the lending institution and person involved, and your name and company. Be sure to put the date of your submission on the same page.

Table of Contents. List, by topic heading, preceded by a roman numeral, the various sections of the document.

Summary. Summarize your data in a page or two. This is optional but highly desirable if the loan request is for a substantial amount or if the document is lengthy (more than eight pages).

Purpose of Loan. Describe what the loan will be used for. Mention precisely where and how the desired funds will be utilized. Also include a table indicating how the loan will be retired.

Income Statement. Present a projected profit-and-loss statement for the forthcoming year together with the actual P&L statements for at least the last two years of operation. This historical data should be provided by the firm's accountant to establish its authenticity.

Balance Sheet. Include balance sheets for the current and previous year. As with the P&L statements, the figures should be provided by an accountant.

Accounts Receivable Aging. List every major item in the firm's accounts receivable and a notation as to whether it is current, over 30, over 60, or over 90 days.

Résumés. List for each of the officers (or key management personnel): name, education (high school, college including major, and graduate school) and work experience.

Exhibits. Include additional financial and other pertinent data.

Finally, make your application professional in appearance

and text. It is worth spending an extra hundred dollars to have a professional editor review your application, making certain that your statements are succinct and grammatically correct. Also, have an expert typist prepare the final document.

2. Adopt the Lender's Point of View

Armed with your polished application, you are ready to approach the lender. As in all sales presentations, you should now try to look at the transaction from his or her point of view. In the case of a bank, for instance, you know that the three important needs are to lend money that provides the greatest security to the bank, to lend money at the maximum yield (highest interest rate), and to obtain additional deposits, so that the bank can make more loans. Your presentation should convince the bank that it's doing itself a favor by granting your loan—a secure, safe, and profitable investment for the bank, in other words.

Don't forget: If you are a new account, you have created a new depositor, which increases the amount of money the bank has on hand. In addition, the bank also gains the "float"—that is, the funds that are in its possession until the checks you have written clear the Federal Reserve Bank. Consequently, it's a good idea to emphasize the approximate size of the balance you plan to maintain in your checking account. For example, if you require a $200,000 line of credit and you normally have a $20,000 balance in your checking account, this 10 percent—called the "compensating balance"—becomes a definite selling point. Some firms will maintain a balance of 20 percent. Some banks require such a compensating balance for certain types of loans. If the bank to whom you are applying for a loan does not require a compensating balance, indicate that you would be maintaining a checking account at that bank with a reasonable minimum balance.

You might also add that some of your employees will likely have checking accounts with the company bank. Your employees will probably generate short-term automobile loans, which are very profitable for the bank. Finally, you may be maintaining a payroll account with the bank, which will provide added float funds.

3. Selecting a Specific Lender

The type of loan that you desire often determines the type of lender that you should seek. Generally, unsecured loans are obtained from banks, private placements, and equity investors. Secured loans come from banks, SBAs, insurance companies, and commercial finance companies. To find the type of lender best suited to your needs, it's often a good idea to get the advice of a financial consultant or acquisition broker.

Once you know which type of lender you desire, how do you select a specific institution? Let's take an example using banks, as they are the prime source of borrowed funds. Approach the bank that is geographically closest to you, all other things being equal. This will provide you with a greater opportunity for frequent, impromptu meetings and for face-to-face contacts.

Approach a bank suited to you in size. Generally a smaller company should work with a smaller bank and a medium-size company should work with a medium-size bank. The smaller, independent banks are usually the easiest to work with because their officers have a broader scope of duties. However, if you are a "fast growth" type of company and you want to make acquisitions or bank contacts in other cities or plan to sell overseas, then work with one of the larger banks in your area.

Select a bank with the capacity to meet your lending requirements. Most banks have a rule that they cannot lend more than 10 percent of the bank's capital to one customer. For example, if a bank has $3 million and a 10 percent loan ceiling, then the maximum you could borrow would be $300,000. Many banks have a financial statement available in the lobby.

Choose a bank where there is a compatible individual available to handle your account. If you don't feel that your personality and the loan officer's match, then be careful. Personalities do have an effect on banking relationships, just as they do in business and employment relationships.

4. Following Through

Once the desired funds have been obtained, it goes without saying that you must make every effort to meet your scheduled payments as agreed.

Idea #90:   You should also make every effort to keep the lending institution adequately informed as to how your business is progressing.

The word "adequately" is the key. Do not overburden the officer with operating information on your firm, but don't keep him or her in the dark about your activities either. Submit a balance so that the officer will be familiar with your activities and will have enough confidence in the investment to help you when unexpected problems arise.

In many large and medium-size businesses a member of the lending institution is often included on the board of directors. But in small, privately owned companies, this is usually not the case, mainly because the board exerts little or no influence on business decisions. In any event, it's prudent to keep in touch with the lender on a regular basis.

Now you have the money, ideas, and techniques to accelerate your growth by means of modern marketing techniques. How do you put it all together? That's the subject of the next chapter.

CHAPTER 12

Now It's Up to You!

"There is nothing permanent except change."

The Greek philosopher Heraclitus said that 2,500 years ago. We of the twentieth century can testify to its enduring truth. The pace of change has accelerated exponentially in our lifetime. It is the single most important element to be considered in our thoughts about the future and, surely, in developing plans for new business opportunities.

Growth involves change. The phrase "growing pains" expresses the fundamental fact that change can be uncomfortable, even wrenching. That's why we often have to fight off our tendency to resist change. Emotionally we need the security that comes from settled and predictable patterns of life. But in planning to accelerate the growth of your business, it's necessary to understand the deep-seated human resistance to new products, new markets, new ways of doing things.

> **Idea #91: The inevitability of change provides new business opportunities. To take advantage of those opportunities, however, you must overcome the natural resistance to change in yourself, your associates, and your public.**

Indeed, a marketing-minded business person is always aware that products come and go. So do markets. Nothing stands still. Products that were once household words drop out of sight. New products arise, sometimes creating totally new industries. The development of integrated circuits gave birth to minicomputers, which answered the need for computer-power in hundreds of areas previously excluded. Prices dropped as sales volumes rose, making minicomputers even more widely available. Then came the development of silicon chips etched with microscopic circuitry. Hand calculators and microcomputers flooded the market, becoming less expensive and easier to use by the month. In creating the computer age, integrated circuits and microdot chips have spawned hundreds of new companies and thousands of new jobs through the ripple effect.

Of course, the process of change works in the opposite direction, too. Products that once boomed fade away. Marketing experts often speak of a product's "life cycle." This is a useful term that recognizes that products, like people and organizations, proceed through identifiable evolutionary phases. "The shadow of market decline and obsolescence is never very far away," a marketing specialist warns ominously.*

PRODUCT LIFE CYCLE

Marketers trace a product's life cycle through five stages, shown in Figure 12-1. The stages are fixed; they are inevitable. What differs is the time that each stage encompasses. Like people, some products live longer—and have more vigorous and successful lives—than others. (Incidentally, it should be mentioned that services share the same fate as products. Marketers often use the word "product" to mean whatever is bought and sold.) A product may last for only a single season, as the "Pet Rock," a 1975 Christmas bonanza, did, or for many years, as Ivory Soap has done. And sometimes products disappear, only to re-emerge later in a slightly different form. Take snuff, for example. In the early 1900s textile

---

* "Your Product's Life Cycle," *Business Monthly*, June 1974, p. 1.

Figure 12-1.   Product life cycle.

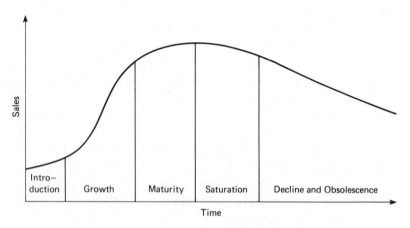

workers commonly used snuff to mask out the putrid aroma of their work environment and to prevent, they thought, tuberculosis. Today, snuff is experiencing something of a comeback. Sales have increased markedly in recent years, probably because of the publicity linking smoking to cancer and heart disease. Unlike cigarettes, snuff can be advertised on television.

Think about your product in terms of its prospective life cycle. Try to determine the stage it's in at present. This kind of thinking may give you the perspective you need to make sound business decisions. Does a recent dip in sales indicate that the product is hopelessly over the hill? Or can the product be revitalized, with renewed marketing efforts? If your product is entering the fifth stage, "decline and obsolescence," perhaps you should become reconciled to its fate and invest your attention and funds elsewhere. Let's examine each stage of the product life cycle in detail.

Introduction

During the first stage buyer demand must be created and the customer must be educated about the superior features of the product. That's why the stage is usually characterized by high promotional costs, high prices, low sales volume, and minimal profits, if any. This is primarily an investment stage.

In general, for a potentially successful new product, there are few competitors at this point. The key factors that will determine success are accurate market research to pinpoint probable customers, sound product design and "debugging," and promotional expertise.

Growth

The growth stage is characterized by the entry of competitors and a scramble for competitive position. These latecomers either did not have the imagination to develop the new product or service in the first place or elected not to risk its introduction.

Advertising strategy shifts from "Try this new product," to "Buy my brand." Sales and profits increase rapidly, but prices and margins-per-unit begin to decline. Distribution and promotional support to lock up market share during this phase are essential.

Maturity

As the product and the market mature, marginal competitors are "shaken out," and a volatile competitive situation may emerge between the survivors, particularly if the item is a consumer product. While sales continue to rise, the pressures of competition increase so that overall profits flatten out or decline. The ability to adapt to this competitive situation and to innovate with new applications for or special models of the product is essential.

Idea #92:   A product's life cycle can be extended in the mature phase by new packaging, repricing, or redesigning for specialty applications.

Jello and Scotch Tape, two classically mature products, have had their lives extended through continual product modifications and new applications. If you have a sick product or product line, however, don't invest the funds and time in it that could be devoted to a healthy item. Often, abandoning old products is as important as introducing new ones.

Saturation

During saturation, total market penetration is reached by the combined efforts of the competitors. Sales begin to be more responsive to basic economic forces, such as recession or inflation, than to promotional expenditure. With sales peaking and profits declining, production efficiencies become a vital competitive factor.

Decline and Obsolescence

It now becomes a question of how long to milk the product before dropping it. Although margins are lowest during these phases, competition has lessened and promotional expenditures can be reduced. With prudent management, a product can sometimes be nursed along for many years with quite satisfactory profits. Lydia E. Pinkham's famous patent medicine "for female complaints," for example, continued to sell with moderate success for many years after the public's faith in such nineteenth-century nostrums had pretty much evaporated.

> **Idea #93: Don't discard a seemingly "obsolete" product without first exploring thoroughly its market potential. See if you can give it new life. Remember, it took a long time for that product to gain acceptance; it will probably take even longer for it to die.**

Change and Your Product's Life Cycle

At what stage is your product in the life cycle? The answer to this question is important because each phase demands different marketing techniques and strategies. The fundamental point is that as an owner or sales manager you are constantly adapting to changing conditions, using all the pertinent aspects of a comprehensive marketing program discussed throughout this book.

How can you be sure that your marketing program is comprehensive enough to cover all situations? Here's a review checklist. Use it for planning and guidance as you adapt the ideas and strategies set forth here.

YOUR MARKETING PROGRAM—A REVIEW

Marketing Strategy

_____ Do you have a written five-year growth plan?

_____ Do you have a short-range marketing budget for the next fiscal year? The budget should contain:

- Specific gross and net sales objectives broken down into monthly quota figures.
- Profit quotas (that is, gross margin targets for each salesperson and for each product line).
- A marketing expense budget listing all major items of expense.

Such a program doesn't have to be elaborate, but it should be in written form. Placing these objectives and plans on paper will provide an aura of commitment and importance.

Customer Relations

_____ Do you know what your *major* customers (the 10 to 20 percent that provide 70 to 80 percent of your business) think about the following?

- The effectiveness of the goods and services you currently provide in comparison with those afforded by your major competitors.
- Their forthcoming needs for new or altered products, which could provide an opportunity for you either to increase sales or to develop new products or services.

_____ Do you meet with key customers regularly? How strong are the relationships between their personnel and your outside and inside sales employees? Are you personally acquainted with at least *two* people at each of these accounts in case one leaves or in case your key salesperson joins a competitor?

_____ Do any one or two single customers represent a disproportionately large portion of your business (more than 15 percent each)?

_____ Are such major customers using their large share of business to pressure you in any way? How stable are these companies in terms of financial and management strengths? Might they be ripe to sell out or merge with another company (which could cause you future problems)?

Sales Employees

Next to customers, your sales employees are probably your most valuable asset as they *are* your company in the eyes of your customers.

_____ Are your outside sales personnel increasing dollar sales and gross margin profits at a rate faster than inflation?

_____ Are your salespeople motivated? Are they enthusiastic?

_____ Are they increasing your market share?

_____ Are their selling and product knowledge skills improving?

_____ Is personnel turnover more than 10 percent a year? If so, why? Is your compensation program serving as a recognized incentive?

_____ Are your inside sales personnel content with their lot in life? Or do they complain about being treated as second-class citizens by the outside sales force?

_____ Are salespeople satisfied with their compensation (amount and incentive)? Do your best inside people yearn to go outside simply because they think they can earn more money?

_____ If you use reps, how important is your firm and its products to them in comparison to their other lines? How do *they* rate your support in comparison to that provided by their other principals? Are the reps producing?

Sales or Marketing Manager

How well is this individual balancing the dual responsibilities of inside administrative paperwork versus outside field work? A field sales manager should spend an average of three to four days a week on the road, an in-house sales manager should spend two to three days a week out of the office, and a marketing manager should be in the field at least one day a week.

Idea #94:   To get your sales or marketing manager to spend more time in the field, make time in the field a factor in the performance review. Base salary increases on this review.

_____   Do you have a performance review session twice a year with your sales or marketing manager covering sales performance against budget and the following field responsibilities?

- Leading salespeople in pursuit of new business.
- Maintaining desired sales productivity among individual salespeople.
- Training and motivating direct and/or rep sales force.
- Maintaining personal contact with key accounts.
- Reporting on competitive activities and new product suggestions.

_____   Is your home office:

- Providing the sales force with sales leads?
- Making certain that proposals, quotations, and literature are sent promptly to prospects?
- Resolving customer and prospect problems?
- Planning and forecasting sales?
- Monitoring sales expenses?
- Working expeditiously on other projects as assigned?

Sales Leads

_____ Are you funding an effective program for developing sales leads? Are your salespeople using these leads to contact new prospects? Are they spending at least a day each week visiting these prospects?

_____ Do you have adequate new case study and product literature being printed periodically so that your direct salesperson or representative has something new to show regular customers?

_____ Do inside salespeople telephone smaller accounts that are not visited regularly? Have you considered a monthly or quarterly newsletter as another means of keeping in touch with accounts?

_____ Is your space advertising in such business publications as *Thomas Register*, the Yellow Pages, and others producing sales leads? If not, should these ads be redesigned or discontinued?

_____ Do your salespeople spend an excessive amount of time in the office? Is it because they are failing to receive the clerical or production support needed to satisfy their customer requirements?

Product Policy

_____ Have you made improvements in your major product line? Have you added new features that will increase the value of your product to major sub-market prospects?

_____ Do you regularly adjust your pricing to cover inflation and other increased manufacturing costs? How does this new pricing position your product or service with respect to your competition?

_____ What new products are planned for release next year? Is their development on schedule? Have you started to plan in detail for the new product introductions (news releases, trade show displays, and product literature) *while allowing ample time to test your product in the field prior to taking the first order?*

_____ Have you reviewed your product line for unprofitable items or for items whose sales are being seriously eroded by competition? Should such products be removed from the line?

_____ Have you thought about bringing out a lower quality, less expensive line to supplement your current offerings? Or should you consider adding a more expensive, higher quality line to the one you now sell?

_____ Are you adequately promoting your old-line products, or are you simply leaving them alone and unattended? Remember, they may be "old" to you, but unknown to prospects!

_____ Do you have a group of employees who meet regularly to discuss potential new products and the updating of old products? How effective are these meetings? How can they be improved?

Distribution

_____ Are your current distribution channels providing maximum market penetration? Is your actual sales spread in proportion to the potential that exists for each area (as defined by SIC county statistics)? What do you plan to do about those areas that are undeveloped?

_____ Have you carefully examined the opportunities of selling to the government (federal, state, or municipal) and overseas?

_____ Have you considered using more than one channel of distribution? Possibly you could sell direct, OEM through distribution, and under private label, all simultaneously!

_____ What are your thoughts about having more than one dealer or distributor in a given geographic area? Have dealers or distributors increased or decreased in their importance in marketing your type of product over the past five to ten years?

_____ Are your dealers and distributors being properly motivated? Are your sales personnel aggressively contacting them? Are they, in turn, actively selling and servicing your

products? Are you generally satisfied with their performance collectively and individually?

Competition

_____ Are any of your competitors gaining market share faster
than your firm? If so, why?

_____ In what market direction are your most capable competitors headed? New products, services, new approaches?
Why? Should you be following their lead or pursuing a
different course of action?

_____ What tangible selling features (product, service, price, or
delivery) do you have to offer that will differentiate you
from your competition in the eyes of the buyer? Are you
fully exploiting these features?

Training

As a company grows and is to continue growing, the owner
is faced with a difficult decision. Should he or she upgrade the
supervisory workforce by bringing in new people with the desired
experience or by training the current supervisory staff? If you elect
to pursue the latter route:

_____ Do you have a management by objective (MBO) program
in effect?

_____ Are you encouraging your supervisors to attend night
school and various training programs?

_____ How are you developing _yourself_ as a manager and
innovator?

Perennial Problems

_____ Are you planning to sweep the following annoying problems under the rug again this year or will you deal with
them directly?

• Performance reviews for everyone on a semi-annual or annual basis.

- Inside salespeople who want to be transferred to field sales.
- Larger discounts for the biggest customers.
- Employees who are no longer earning their pay, because they are too old, ineffective, unmotivated, or dissatisfied.
- Employees who continually ask for a Christmas party, an extra holiday, their relatives to be hired, or the bathroom to be repainted!
- Employees who would like to know about advancement opportunities with your firm, and to whom you have nothing to say.
- Customers whose complaints you haven't answered.

Idea #95: If one of your key employees leaves you to work for a competitor and takes some of your ideas and customers with him, don't waste time or expense on a costly lawsuit unless your claim is very substantial.

THE GREAT EXECUTIVE

Idea #96: Great chief executives know what they don't know.

This is an often unrecognized but common characteristic of successful businessmen that I have noted in my 12 years as a marketing consultant. An owner of any business wears many hats. He or she cannot be an expert in all or even most of the elements involved in running a growing business: sales, sales promotion, advertising, accounting, law, automation, data processing, production, product design, personnel, recruitment, planning, pricing, and market research. This is a formidable list but it doesn't begin to cover all the areas of expertise required.

No one is expected to know everything in so complex a matter as running a successful business. My idea of a great executive is one who is able to recognize and admit to a lack of knowledge in a given business situation. Such a person can correctly assess the relative importance of that situation and will spend the money to engage the talent to fill the gaps in knowledge. The great executive also knows how to find the people with the necessary talent.

> **Idea #97:   The decisions on how to resolve a business problem are usually not difficult to make if the decision maker has assembled complete and accurate information on which to base the decisions.**

BECOME AS BIG AS YOU WANT TO BE

Business owners often ask me how large a company they can build. My reply, invariably, is: "You can build as large a business as you want, provided you are able and willing to invest the personal time and take the necessary financial risks."

> **Idea #98:   To build a large business, you must think big and be prepared to take risks.**

If you plan to build a $50 million business, your attitude and approach must be quite different from what it would be if you seek to build a $500,000 business. You would probably have to work harder, for one thing. On a recent plane trip I read an article about a businessman who had worked 16 hours a day, seven days a week, for five years. At the end of that time he was worth over $1 million. Not surprising!

I don't really believe that you have to be a workaholic to succeed, though. I doubt if excessive work habits figure importantly in the lifestyles of most great executives. One characteristic I've often noticed among successful business people is an outgoing personality. It may not be essential, but it certainly helps!

> **Idea #99:   Every successful business owner has to sell— all the time.**

Not only does the owner have to sell the company's products, he or she has to sell ideas as well. And the owner has to sell everyone on those ideas: employees, bankers, community leaders, vendors and suppliers, business associates, and usually one's spouse! Fortunately, oral expression is not the only way to sell. The written word can be an excellent sales tool for those who aren't exceptional talkers.

And even if you lack an outgoing personality or a flair for writing, you can be an effective salesperson by simply *listening*. Often thoughtful sensitivity toward the wants and needs of others can be far more effective than oral fireworks and flamboyance.

Idea #100:   Be yourself! It's not brashness that really sells, but sincerity and understanding.

YOU CAN MAKE IT WORK!

This book is a roadmap to the principles and practices of marketing, derived from my experience as a business consultant. We've covered the whole field, from market research to funding an acquisition. The stress has been on growth, *accelerated* growth, by use of the tools provided in a comprehensive marketing program. I've seen these approaches help my clients. I'm sure they can help you, too.

Naturally every principle and every idea will not apply to your particular situation or to the marketing problems you may be facing at the time you read this book. The idea is to extract those that can work for you now. Keep this book for further reference when new problems arise or when you're ready to explore new avenues of growth through the marketing concepts set forth here.

Idea #101:   Act now. Time is your major resource. Don't let it escape!

The rest is up to you. Good luck!

Index

*Accounting Firms and Practition-
ers* (American Institute of
Certified Public Accountants),
168
accounts, analysis of, 5
acquisitions
funding, 187–188
negotiating for, 183–187
preparation for, 165–167
screening, 171–176
searching for, 167–171
value of potential, 176–183
Admore Company, founding of,
4–5
advertising
for acquisitions, 171
articles as, 135–136
brochures as, 137–140
cost effectiveness of, 5
differentiation with, 50
direct mail as, 127–133
in directories and publications,
121–122
as marketing technique, 5–6, 10
new products, 122–124
for salespeople, 85–87, 92
space, 136–137
in Yellow Pages, 119–121

advertising agencies, use of, 122
Albee-Campbell, Inc., 93
Alice in Wonderland (Carroll),
24–25
American Institute of Certified
Public Accountants, directory
of, 168
American Management Associa-
tions, and management train-
ing, 101–102
on sales compensation, 94,
96–97
American Marketing Association,
as information source, 15,
104
American Telephone & Telegraph
Company, 127
Amos Tuck School of Business,
102
"Analyzing New Product Risk,"
*Marketing for Sales Execu-
tives,* 150–151
annual sales forecast, 28–30
Annual Statement Studies (Robert
Morris Associates), 179
Annual Survey of Manufacturers
(Department of Commerce),
22

Anthony J. Zinno Associates, 93
Arthur D. Little (consultants), 54
articles, self-promotional,
    135–136
A.T. Kearney, Inc., 150–151
attrition of customer base,
    118–119

Back Scratchers Club, 93
banks, see commercial banks
Berlyn Corporation, 125
board of directors, growth-minded
    38–40
Boston Envelope Company, The,
    and market definition, 26
Bobrow, Edwin, 93–94, 95
Booze, Allen & Hamilton (con-
    sultants), 54
borrowing
    preparing for, 197–200
    see also loans
Boston Tennis Center, 14
brochures, self-promotional,
    137–140
budget, projecting, 27–30
Bureau of the Budget, as market-
    ing research source, 23,
    76–77
Bureau of Census, as marketing
    research source, 15, 76–77
business owner
    characteristics of, 213–215
    goal-setting for, 26–27
    training, 101–103
Business Periodicals Index (BPI),
    21
business plan, see game plan
business seminars, 102
Business Week, 135
buyer differentiation, 50–51
buyer segments, indentifying, 3
    see also customers

capital
    borrowing, 191–201

equity, acquiring, 189–190
Carlson, Walter O., on sales com-
    pensation, 94, 96–97
Caswell, Robert on Yellow Pages
    ads, 120–121
Census of Manufacturers (Depart-
    ment of Commerce), 22
census, national, as marketing re-
    search source, 15, 21–22
Characteristics of the Population
    (Department of Commerce),
    15
Chartier, Ray (president, Standard
    Duplicator Sales), 25
closing techniques, in sales,
    63–64
collateral, defining, 194
Commerce Business Daily (De-
    partment of Commerce), 160
commercial banks
    borrowing from, 191–193, 200
    and buyer segments, 3
commissions, for sales reps, 94,
    96–98, 109
compensation techniques, for
    sales reps, 94–98, 107
competition, evaluating, 212
consumer behavior, identifying,
    12–24
consumer market, identifying,
    12–19
consumer research services, as in-
    formation source, 15–18
cooperative buying organizations,
    using, 67–68
corporate call report (CCR), 114,
    115–116
cost effectiveness, of advertising,
    5
Cotter & Company, 67
County Business Patterns (Depart-
    ment of Commerce), 22,
    76–77
credibility gap, closing, in sales,
    60–63

Cross-Newform (manufacturer), 162

"Cup Lids for the Use of Teabags and the Like," as example of useless product, 6–7

customer file, as source of industrial market data, 20–21

customer installation, use of, in sales, 61

customers
attrition of, 113–114
market research as defining, 11–24
needs of, defining, 6–9
new, finding, 3–4, 157–161
as prospects, 125–133
relations with, 207–208
sorting out, 3

Dale Carnegie, training courses of, 103

data source firms, for industrial market information, 24

Dartmouth College, 102

Davner, Jack, on sales compensation, 94, 96–97

dealers, using, 66–68

decision maker, in selling process, 57–59

delivery, as element of differentiation, 51–52

demonstration, of product, 61–63

Department of Agriculture, as information source, 22

Department of Commerce
as marketing research source, 15, 21–22
and overseas markets, 161

Department of Labor, as marketing research source, 22

Diamond, William T., on sales reps, 71, 73–74

differentiation, as marketing strategy, 41–55

Digital Equipment Corporation, 43

direct mail, as marketing technique, 6, 127–133

Direct Mail (S.D. Warren Co., publisher), 128

Direct Marketing and Response System (DMARS), 127

directories, as market research sources, 22–24

Directory of Directories, 23

Directory of New England Manufacturing (George D. Hall, publisher), 22

Directory of U.S. and Canadian Marketing Surveys Services, 23

display, of new product, 47–48

distribution
as marketing element, 9
strategy, in selling process, 68–74, 211–212

Distribution Channels for Industrial Goods (Diamond), 71, 73–74

distributors
and differentiation, 53–54
hiring, 94
using, 66–68, 71–74

diversification, *see* internal diversification; external diversification

Doriot, George S., on hiring, 92

Dun & Bradstreet
marketing services of, 167–168, 174
publications of, 22–23, 76, 126–127

Eagle Electric Supply Company, 52

Economic Information Systems, 76–77

electronic piano tuner, 44, 45

Emerson, Ralph Waldo, 1

employment ads, placing, 85

employment agencies, using, 86–87

Encyclopedia of Associations, The, 21

Engineering Sales Corporation (ENSACO), 57–58, 59, 104

equity capital, acquiring, 189–190

expansion of services, as marketing approach, 4–5

external diversification, 164–188

federal government, as new market, 159–160

Findex, 23

Find/SVP (data source firm), 24

focus groups, in consumer sampling, 17–18

follow-up service, as element in differentiation, 10, 52–53

Food and Drug Administration, 45

Fortune, 135

Foundry Technology, Inc., 52

game plan, making a, 25–38

General Electric Corporation

and marketing error, 7

Research and Development Department of, 155n.

General Electronic Services, 51

General Learning (firm), failure of, 7

geographic approach, to sales territories, 78–80

give-aways, as self-promotion technique, 141, 148

Gloucester Company

founding of, 3–4

packaging success of, 48

goal-setting, as step preliminary to selling, 24–38

GSA Supply Catalog (Government Printing Office), 160

Guide to Industrial Statistics (Department of Commerce), 21–22

Hall, George D. (publisher), 22

Hamblet, Jim (president, Foundry Technology, Inc.), 52

Hanlon, Al

and buyer differentiation, 51

founder of Admore Company, 4–5, 124

Harvard Business School, 25, 92, 103

Heraclitus, on change, 202

Herring Curtis (founder, Gloucester Company), 3–4

Hofer, John, marketing techniques of, 5–6

horizontal integration, 150

Horka, Al (president, Plastic Extrusion and Engineering Company), 45–46

house accounts, and sales reps, 97–98

IBM, and modified product approach, 151

image, creating a good, 133–148

Income Opportunities, 93

industrial market, identifying, 13, 20–24

industrial products, pricing of, 49

industry approach, to sales territories, 80–81

Information Industry Association (data source firm), 24

Information On Demand (data source firm), 24

information sources, for marketing research, 15–24

intermediaries, in acquisitions process, 168, 170

internal diversification, 149–163

International Directory of Marketing Research Houses and

Services (American Marketing Association), 15, 18
interviews, job, conducting, 88–90
inventions, *see* products, new
Ivory Soap, 203

Jello, 205
job description, for salespeople, 82–83, 84
Johnson & Johnson, marketing strategy of, 41
journals, trade
advertising in, 121–122, 135–136
as information source, 21

Kinkead, Michael, on marketing niche, 42–43
Krazy Glue, as modified product, 151
Krentzman, Chet (Boston deal-maker), 185

Landon, Alf, 16
letter of transmittal, in acquisitions process, 168, 169
letters, in direct mail campaigns, 130–133
line cards, self-promotional, 137–140
Literary Digest, election prediction of, 16–17
loan application, elements of, 197–199
loans
preparation for acquiring, 197–200
selecting a lender for, 200
sources of, 191–197
location of market, *see* market areas
Lombardi, Vince, on sales, 82
long-range plan
examples of, 31–35
making a, 30–38

mail, direct, *see* direct mail
mailing list, for direct mail campaign, 128–130
maintenance, as element of differentiation, 52–53
manufacturers' agents, using, 66–68, 71, 72–73
Manufacturers' Agents National Association (MANA), directory of, 92
Manufacturers' Agents Newsletter, Inc., 93
Manville, Richard, 17n.
market areas, defining, 4, 26
marketing
approaches to, 3–6
defined, 2
elements of, listed, 9–10
misconceptions of, 6–9
research, 11–24
strategy, 207
marketing manager, evaluating, 209
Marketing Through Manufacturers' Agents (Bobrow), 93–94, 95
market niche, as element of differentiation, 42–43
market research and planning
basic questions of, 18–19
and consumer market, 12–19
defined, 9
examples of, 11–14
and industrial market, 20–24
information sources for, 15–24
markets, new, developing, 157–163
Markoa Corporation, 110
Million Dollar Directory (Dun & Bradstreet), 22–23, 76, 126–127
Mister Party, Inc., marketing approach of, 12–13
Moody's *Industrial Manual*, 23
motivation, sales, 107–110

mousetrap, better, as fallacy, 1–2,
    7, 162

National Cash Register Company,
    53
National Council of Salesmen's
    Organizations, Inc., 93
*National Trade and Professional
    Associations of the United
    States and Canada & Labor
    Unions, The,* 21
new concepts, exposure to, 27
New England Business, 122
New England Telephone Com-
    pany, 120
newspapers, advertising in, 5, 92,
    171
new product releases, 122–124
New Products Planning Commit-
    tee, function of, 153–156
New York Times, The, 92

objectives, setting, as step prelim-
    inary to selling, 24–38
obsolescence, product, 206
opinion polls, *see* surveys
overseas markets, developing,
    160–161
owner, *see* business owner

packaging, as selling tool, 46–49
Paragon Steel Corporation, 118
"peer competition program," 110,
    111
periodicals, trade, as information
    source, 21
personnel agencies, using, *see*
    employment agencies
"Pet Rock," 203
Phenoseal
    development of, 3–4
    packaging of, 48
Phillips, Van, on motivating
    salespeople, 110, 111
Pinkham, Lydia E., 206

planning, as step preliminary to
    selling, 24–38
Plastic Extrusion and Engineering
    Company (PEXCO), 45–46
Predicasts, 21, 175
Predicasts, Inc., 21
pricing
    as element of differentiation,
        49–50
    strategy, for new products,
        156–157
Pringles Potato Chips, 153
Procter & Gamble, 28, 49, 153
product policy, 210–211
products, new
    defining, 4, 6–9
    demonstrating, 61–63
    development of, 9, 204–205
    differentiation of, 44–46
    ideas for, 153–156
    introducing, to new market,
        161–163
    introducing, to present market,
        152–153
    life cycle of, 203–207
    packaging of, 46–49
    pricing, 156–157
    releases on, 122–124
    risks of, 37–38
    and salespeople training,
        105–107
products, present
    life cycle of, 203–207
    modification of, 151–152,
        205–206
    and new market, 157–161
    obsolescence of, 206
product sheet, example of, 8
promotion, as element of differen-
    tiation, 50
proposals
    sample of, 142–147
    as selling tool, 140–141
prospect report, monthly hot-,
    114, 116

prospects, identifying, 126–133
publications
    advertising in, 121–122,
        135–136
    as marketing research sources,
        15–24
public relations campaign,
        133–148
public speaking, self-promotional,
        136
purchase-sale agreement, for new
        acquisition, 185–187
purchasing agents
    self-promotion and, 141, 148
    in selling process, 57–58

"Qualities that Make Salespeople
        Tops," *Sales & Marketing
        Management*, 106
questionnaires, interpretation of,
        16, 19

*Rand-McNally International
        Banker's Directory*, 168
references, checking, 90
referrals, use of, in hiring, 87, 92
repairs, as element of differentia-
        tion, 52–53
representation, choosing, 64–74
research services, consumer, *see*
        consumer research services
Robertson, Jack W., 160
role playing, as sales training
        technique, 104–105
Roosevelt, Franklin D., 16

Saddlebrook Corporation, 43
salaries, for sales reps, 94, 96–98,
        109
sales, as marketing element, 10
Sales & Marketing Management,
        surveys of, 76, 105, 106, 160
Sales Executive Club of New
        York, 81

Sales Marketing Executives of
        Chicagor, 110
sales forecast, *see* annual sales
        forecast
sales leads, generating, 118–133,
        210
sales levels, increasing, 27–38
sales manager, evaluating, 209
Salesmark
    annual report of, 36
    sales data of, 69–70
salespeople, direct
    compensation for, 94
    controlling, 110–116
    evaluating, 208–209
    hiring, 82–94
    motivating, 107–110
    terminating, 98–99
    territories of, 78–80
    training of, 100, 103–107
    using, 65–73
sales presentations, making,
        60–63
sales progress, monitoring, 30–37
sales projections, *see* annual sales
        forecast
sales representatives
    appointment letter for, 95
    compensation for, 94
    controlling, 110–116
    evaluating, 208–209
    hiring, 92–94
    motivating, 107–110
    terminating, 98–99
    territories of, 77–78
    training of, 100, 103–107
    using, 66–73
sales techniques, developing,
        103–107
sales territories
    for direct salespeople, 78–80
    formula for establishing, 75–78
sampling, *see* surveys
Sanderson, Dr. Albert (Sight-O-
        Tuner inventor), 44

Scotch Tape, 205
Scott Paper Company, 128
screening, as step in hiring, 87–88
S.D. Warren Company, 128
Seaboard Foundry, 162
search firms, using, 86–87
selling process
 closing techniques for, 63–64
 decision maker in, 57–59
 distribution strategy in, 68–74
 representation in, 64–68
 sales presentation in, 60–63
 see also sales techniques
selling spectrum, 43–55
Selling to the Federal Government (Robertson), 160
seminars, business, 101–102
service
 development of, defined, 9
 as element in differentiation,
  44–46
service companies
 and differentiation, 54
 selling techniques for, 64–74
Shriberg, William (manager, General Electronic Services), 52
SIC system, 23–24, 76, 121, 126
Sjogren, Dick (manufacturer),
  126–127
Sjogren Tool and Machine Company, 126–127
Sleicher, Harry (president, Seaboard Foundry), 162
Slutsky, Martin, 1
Small Business Act of 1953,
  194–195
Small Business Administration
  (SBA), 22
 borrowing from, 191, 194–195
Small Business Investment Corporation (SBIC), borrowing
  from, 191, 195–196
Smaller Business Association of
  New England (SBANE), 101
space advertising, 136–137

specifications, for acquisitions,
  165–166
Spectra-Polymer, Inc., long-range
  plan of, 30–35
Standard Duplicator Sales (office
  equipment firm), 25
Standard Industrial Classification
  Manual (Bureau of the
  Budget), 23–24, 76, 79
Standard Industrial Classification
  system, 23–24, 76, 79, 121,
  126, 175
Standard Periodical Directory, 21
statistics
 in consumer surveys, 17
 industrial, obtaining, 21–24
Stayflex (manufacturer), 111
"Steps in Conducting a Marketing
  Research Study" (Manville),
  17n.
stocking representative, see man-
  ufacturers' agent
Stroum, Steve (founder, Venmark
  Corporation), 54
Super-Dry Sure, pricing of, 49
"Survey of Industrial Purchasing
  Power" (Sales & Marketing
  Management), 76
surveys
 consumer, 16–19
 trade and professional, 21
suspects, identifying, 126–133

target marketing group, identifying, 11–24
 see also game plan, making a
Taylor, Thayer C., on establishing
  sales territories, 75–78
telemarketing, 127
telephone, using, to screen prospects, 127
Thomas Register, 23
Time, Inc., and marketing error, 7
trade financing, 196
Trade Shows in the Marketing

Mix (Hanlon), 124
Tosdale, Professor Harry R., on
   sales compensation, 94,
   96–97
trade shows, objectives of,
   124–125
training of salespeople, 100–107,
   212
Tranti Systems, 53, 58
True Value,® (cooperative buying
   organization), 67
Tuners Supply Company, 44

underpricing, as marketing tech-
   nique, 5
U.S. Army, 18
U.S. Bureau of Census, *see* Bu-
   reau of Census
U.S. Bureau of the Budget, *see*
   Bureau of the Budget
U.S. Department of Agriculture,
   see Department of Agriculture
U.S. Department of Labor, *see* De-
   partment of Labor
*U.S. Government Purchasing and
   Sales Directory* (SBA), 160

value, ascertaining, of potential
   acquisition, 176–183
Venmark Corporation, 54
*Verified Directory of Manufactur-
   ers' Agents,* 93
vertical integration, 150

Voice (National Council of Sales-
   men's Organizations), 93
Volk, Gerald (president of Tuners
   Supply Company), 44

Wall Street Journal, The, 92, 135,
   171
Warner-Edison Associates (data
   source firm), 24
Warren, Philip, on attrition, 118,
   119
*Washington Information Work-
   book* (Washington Researchers), 160
Washington Researchers (consulting firm), 160
weekly call report (WCR),
   111–113
Whiting, Percy, on selling, 59
wholesalers, *see* distributors

Xerox Learning Systems, 103

Yellow Pages
   advertising in, 5, 12, 119–121,
      136, 175, 176
   business brokers in, 168
   research services in, 15, 18
   sales reps in, 93
   sales trainers in, 104

zip codes, and sales territories, 79